GROSSET & DUNLAP

Published by the Penguin Group

Penguin Group (USA) LLC, 375 Hudson Street, New York, New York 10014, USA

USA | Canada | UK | Ireland | Australia | New Zealand | India | South Africa | China

penguin.com

A Penguin Random House Company

Written by Cavan Scott and Brandon T. Snider

© 2015 Activision Publishing, Inc. Skylanders Universe is a trademark and Activision is a registered trademark of Activision Publishing, Inc. Published by Grosset & Dunlap, a division of Penguin Young Readers Group, 345 Hudson Street, New York, New York 10014. GROSSET & DUNLAP is a trademark of Penguin Group (USA) LLC.
Manufactured in China.

ISBN 978-0-448-48039-8   10 9 8 7 6 5 4 3 2 1

THE COMPLETE COLLECTION

Grosset & Dunlap
An Imprint of Penguin Group (USA) LLC

Contents

Introduction		5
Air Skylanders		7
Earth Skylanders		33
Fire Skylanders		59
Life Skylanders		85
Magic Skylanders		111
Tech Skylanders		137
Undead Skylanders		163
Water Skylanders		189
Checklists		215
Index		222

FROZEN IN OUR WORLD. ALIVE IN THEIRS.

When the Skylanders were banished from Skylands, it didn't just change everything in their world; it also changed everything in ours.

Defeated in battle by the evil Kaos, the heroic Skylanders were sucked through time and space to a bewildering alien planet. That planet was Earth! It didn't help matters for the Skylanders that they were also frozen solid, unable to make their way home.

But help was at hand in the form of the next generation of Portal Masters . . . you! Using the ancient and mystical Portal of Power, you can bring the Skylanders to life and transport them back to Skylands, where a rematch with Kaos awaits. Once home, with a little help from you and their ethereal mentor, Master Eon, the Skylanders can set about restoring peace to their incredible realm of floating islands.

WHO ARE THE SKYLANDERS?

Only the bravest, smartest, fastest, and strongest residents of Skylands were selected by Eon to join his band of heroic defenders. Now, for the first time, all of them are shown together in one Leviathan-size guide.

Each Skylander is aligned to one of the eight Elements that combine to fuel their incredible homeland: Air, Earth, Fire, Life, Magic, Tech, Undead, and Water. In this book, they're divided up by Element, but also by the following five types . . .

 TRAP TEAM Kaos has blown up the walls of the feared Cloudcracker Prison, freeing the most notorious villains in Skylands. It's up to these Trap Team Skylanders to find and capture them using Traptanium, a magic material that can harness the power of the Elements.

 MINIS The Skylander Minis started off assisting the Skylanders on their exciting adventures. Determined to become full-fledged heroes, they trained at Skylanders Academy, honing their powers until they were ready. Now, they stand side by side with their full-grown counterparts, ready to defend Skylands against evil.

 SKYLANDER These "regular" Skylanders are anything but ordinary. They are the heroes who took on Kaos to defend the Core of Light, then ventured back from exile to rebuild it and save the day.

 GIANTS They're not called Giants for fun; these guys are huge! The Giants first joined forces many moons ago to become the original Skylanders and rise up to defeat the Arkeyan Robot King.

 SWAP FORCE These exceptional Skylanders were once caught in a magical volcanic blast that gifted them the unusual ability to SWAP top and bottom halves. Now they can combine in hundreds of ways to take on evil like never before.

Air

Air Skylanders

Gusto 9

Thunderbolt 10

Breeze 11

Pet-Vac 12

Blades 13

Fling Kong 14

Jet-Vac 15

Lightning Rod 16

Pop Thorn 17

Scratch 18

Sonic Boom 19

Warnado 20

Whirlwind 21

Swarm 22

Boom Jet 23

Boom Jet SWAPs 24-27

Free Ranger 28

Free Ranger SWAPs 29-32

Gusto

Gusts and Glory!

Origin: Gusto mastered the art of cloud wrangling with a little help from his mentor, the mysterious Cloud Dragon. But everything changed in the Thunderclap Kingdom when a band of dragon hunters invaded. Gusto drove the hunters away, protecting the kingdom and saving the Cloud Dragon. That heroic act earned him membership in the Skylanders.

Personality: Gusto is a big guy with a heart of gold. Not *actual* gold, of course, but Gusto's heart is just as precious.

Most likely to: Use his Traptanium Boomerang to kick evil right in the pants.

Least likely to: Run away from danger. Gusto runs *toward* danger.

Thunderbolt

TRAP MASTER

A Storm Is Coming!

Origin: Thunderbolt dreamed of using his legendary Storm Sword to protect his home on Mount Cloudpierce. His dream came true the day a Frost Mage stole the sword and turned Skylands into a winter nightmare. Thunderbolt heroically snatched it back and changed the weather back to normal. His bravery earned him a place on the Skylanders Trap Team.

Personality: Thunderbolt is a fierce competitor who faces each opponent with honor and bravery.

Most likely to: Ride his twin bolts of chained lightning into battle.

Least likely to: Use his Traptanium Storm Sword to make it drizzle. Drizzle is the *worst*.

Twists of Fury!

Breeze

Origin: Breeze is half dragon and half unicorn, just like her mentor, Whirlwind. It can be difficult for Breeze sometimes because she doesn't feel accepted by either species, but now that she's graduated from Skylanders Academy, the sky is the limit!

Personality: When Breeze blows into town—look out! She likes to keep things light and airy but can be a little stubborn from time to time.

Most likely to: Show a pack of Trolls what a Rainbow of Doom looks like!

Least likely to: Meditate. It's too hard to sit still.

MINI

Pet-Vac

Hawk and Awe!

Origin: Whenever Jet-Vac needs a little assistance, he calls his little buddy, Pet-Vac, to help him out. Pet-Vac learned how to use his jet pack by zooming around Skylanders Academy instead of just studying it in a book. Together they're proud to serve as faithful members of the Skylanders.

Personality: Pet-Vac is an honorable soldier who gladly puts the needs of others before himself. His bravery and heroism earned him the respect of his teammates.

Most likely to: Soar as high as the sky will allow.

Least likely to: Take a vacation. He's too busy flying!

Looking
Sharp!

Blades

Origin: Blades faithfully stood watch over the Golden Fear Serpent like his ancestors before him. But after one hundred years of peaceful slumber, the serpent roared back to life. In order to stop the serpent from destroying Scalos Castle, Blades switched places with him and conquered his fears. That brave act earned him membership in the Skylanders.

Personality: Blades is willing to do whatever it takes to protect others from harm. Even if it means sacrificing himself to do it!

Most likely to: Conquer his fears.

Least likely to: Hide in the dungeon when it's storming outside. That place is scary.

Fling Kong

Monkey See, Monkey Doom!

Origin: Fling Kong is a master of Monk-Ru and protector of the ancient monkey idol known as Kubla-Wa. When General Snot and his stinky Gorilla-Goos tried to snatch the golden treasure, Fling Kong used his vortex discs and flying rug to defeat them and save the idol. Master Eon made him a Skylander soon after.

Personality: Fling Kong is no stranger to battle, but he prefers a life of peace. He's committed to his training and is willing to do whatever it takes to fight for what is right.

Most likely to: Use his Monk-Ru air-fighting skills to blow away the competition.

Least likely to: Hang out with a Gorilla-Goo. Those things are gross!

Jet-Vac

SKYLANDER

Hawk and Awe!

Origin: When the forces of Darkness raided the realm of Windham, flying ace Jet-Vac gifted his magical wings to a mother so that she could fly her brood to safety. His act of self-sacrifice so impressed Eon that the Portal Master presented the Sky Baron with a Jet-Vac jet pack so that he could take to the air once again.

Personality: Noble and just, courageous Jet-Vac always thinks of others before himself. Now a Skylander, he soars where even eagles never dare.

Most likely to: Keep a stiff upper beak.

Least likely to: Admit that he's feeling a little ruffled.

Lightning Rod

One Strike and You're Out!

Origin: The greatest champion of the ancient Storm Titans, Lightning Rod eventually grew bored with being worshipped. When Kaos appeared during the annual Storm Games and demanded that the Titans submit to his dark authority, Lightning Rod blasted the wicked Portal Master with a bolt from the blue. An impressed Eon quickly made him a Skylander.

Personality: Charm and charisma personified, Lightning Rod is fully aware of his own monumental talents. He's happy to blow his own horn, but happier still to blast evildoers with thunder and lightning.

Most likely to: Get distracted by his own hunky image in a mirror.

Least likely to: Underestimate himself.

Full Scream Ahead!

Sonic Boom

Origin: Sonic Boom searched Skylands for the tallest mountain on which to build her nest, but even then she couldn't escape from sneaky egg snatchers. Her earsplitting scream sent a wizard egg-collector tumbling from the summit, but not before he placed a curse on her unhatched griffin brood.

Personality: Protective as only a mother can be, Sonic Boom shelters all who need help beneath her wings.

Most likely to: Scream until she's made herself heard.

Least likely to: Lose her voice.

Warnado

SKYLANDER

For the Wind!

Origin: Snatched from his swampy nest by a sentient tornado, this turbulent turtle was hatched in the eye of the storm. The enchanted twister taught Warnado everything it knew about the Air Element. When Warnado finally span out onto terra firma, he was spotted by Whirlwind who introduced him to Eon.

Personality: One of the most powerful Air sorcerers of all time, Warnado is quick-witted and has lightning-fast reflexes.

Most likely to: Work himself into a spin.

Least likely to: Stay still. Standing on solid ground makes Warnado dizzy.

Twists of Fury!

Origin: Half dragon and half unicorn, Whirlwind wasn't accepted by either species until she rained down vengeance on a pack of hunter trolls. Whirlwind descended from her cloudy hideout and sent the trolls flying with a beautiful, but blinding, Rainbow of Doom.

Personality: Graceful but strong-willed, Whirlwind's moods are as changeable as the weather itself—although she tries to keep her stormy temper under control.

Most likely to: Throw caution to the wind and unleash a tempestuous tantrum on her enemies.

Least likely to: Keep a calm head when provoked.

Swarm

Bring the Sting!

Origin: Growing up as a warrior bug prince, Swarm was destined for big things. Very big things. In fact, he never stopped growing. Eventually the titanic insect smashed through the roof of the kingdom's pyramid-shaped honeycomb hive. Supersize Swarm made a beeline for the Skylanders to offer his services as a Giant.

Personality: This immense insect is as adventurous as he is unique. He was the first of his family to buzz off from the hive and become a hero.

Most likely to: Add a barbed insult to a stinging attack.

Least likely to: Get caught short of ideas. He always has a "plan bee" up his sleeve.

Bombs Away!

 SWAP FORCE

Boom Jet

Origin: A complete show-off, Boom Jet could always be found pulling off bodacious moves on his sky-surfboard. But when the Darkness rolled across the Billowy Cloudplains, Boom Jet rose to the challenge, rescuing everyone before their homes were destroyed.

Personality: Daredevil Boom Jet always has to be the best at what he—does and can seem full of himself at times. Luckily, he's as brave as he is boastful.

Most likely to: Push himself further—and faster—every day.

Least likely to: Take a break. Being this perfect takes practice.

Boom Blade

Have skates, will travel!

Boom Bomb

Try out Boom Jet's Tight Spiral attack alongside Stink Bomb's Skunk Cloud.

Boom Buckler

What Boom Jet loses in aerial abilities, he gains in tentacle terror.

The sky-surfer gets magnetized!

Send Boom Jet drilling for victory, with added Coconut Mayhem.

Boom Jet's Football Bomb and Fire Kraken's Sizzling Sparkler, together at last.

A great combo for fans of Boom Jet's Bombers and Hoot Loop's Time Sink.

Boom Ranger

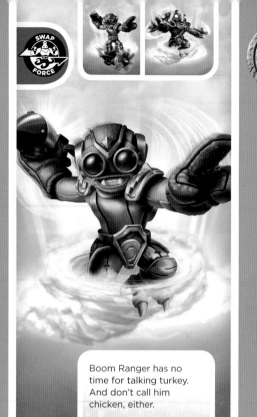

Boom Ranger has no time for talking turkey. And don't call him chicken, either.

Boom Rise

Add climbing ability to Boom Jet's aerial prowess for one seriously versatile Skylander.

Boom Rouser

Take Boom Jet seriously out of his comfort zone—underground!

Boom Shadow

With a mega Go Long throw on top and Shadow Kick down below, this is one powerful mash-up.

Boom Shake

See how Skylands' sky-surfing hero gets to grips with Rattle Shake's Tail Sweep.

Boom Shift

Storm Bomb meets Foggy Movement with this creepy combo.

Boom Stone

Take Boom Jet for a spin and send enemies scattering.

Boom Zone

A burning hot combination of Air and Fire.

Free Ranger

Whip up a Storm!

Origin: Free Ranger fell in love with storms the moment his egg was struck by lightning. As soon as he hatched, he began tracking twisters and charging after cyclones. Luckily, Master Eon saved him before he jumped into the deadliest tempest he'd ever seen—the Darkness itself!

Personality: A real whirlwind, this extreme storm-chaser is sometimes too impetuous for his own good.

Most likely to: Talk about the weather.

Least likely to: Decide to stay indoors 'cause it's raining.

Free Blade

Free Ranger gets his skates on with this Air and Water combo.

Free Bomb

A stinky SWAP gifting Free Ranger Stink Bomb's Skunk-Fu skills.

Free Buckler

Take Free Ranger's top and Wash Buckler's bottom. Just don't get those feathers wet!

Free Charge

Half Storm Chicken.
Half Ultron Robot.
All good!

Free Drilla

Skylands' number one silverback assumes a plucky poultry presence.

Free Jet

This feathered ace takes to the skies with the aid of Boom Jet's sky-surfing Wind Turbine.

Free Kraken

Did someone order the sizzling-hot chicken?

Free Loop

This combination of Air, Magic, feathers, and claws makes for one tough bird.

Free Rise

A chance to combine Free Ranger's Gale Slash with Spy Rise's Spyder Climb.

Free Rouser

Free Ranger's love of the skies and Rubble Rouser's digging dexterity make for an all-terrain assassin.

Free Shadow

Make this SWAP for the perfect mix of bravery and cunning.

31

Free Shake

You would *never* see these two hanging out together in the wild. Or would you?

Free Shift

Night Shift's creepy Float Like a Vampire move transfers across to our storm-chasing chicken.

Free Stone

Take Free Ranger for a Stoney Spin, using Doom Stone's rock-hard gem belt.

Free Zone

An awesome combination of Fire and feather.

Earth

Head Rush 35

Wallop 36

Bop 37

Terrabite 38

Bash 39

Dino-Rang 40

Fist Bump 41

Flashwing 42

Prism Break 43

Rocky Roll 44

Scorp 45

Slobber Tooth 46

Terrafin 47

Crusher 48

Doom Stone 49

Doom Stone SWAPs 50-53

Rubble Rouser 54

Rubble Rouser SWAPs 55-58

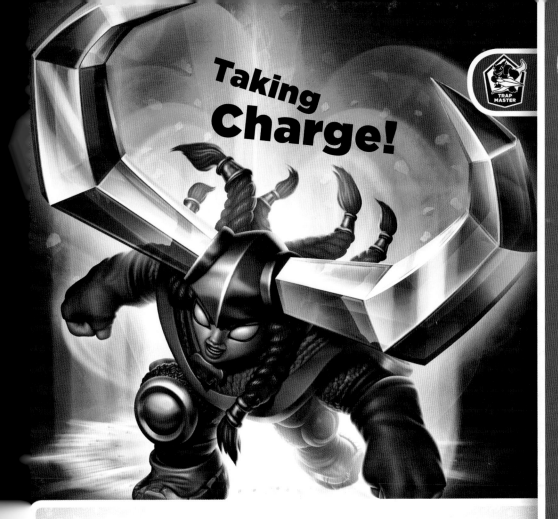

Taking Charge!

Origin: An evil Harvest Sphinx cast a spell upon an unsuspecting village, making the villagers plow the fields of golden grass day and night. Head Rush had to do something to save the day so she let loose an inspirational yodel that woke up her friends and drove the Sphinx away forever. Her bravery earned her membership on the Skylanders Trap Team!

Personality: Head Rush's positive attitude is an inspiration to her friends. She may not think of herself as a great leader, but Master Eon and the Skylanders know she's on a path to greatness.

Most likely to: Use her Traptanium Horns to charge into battle.

Least likely to: Sit in a field of golden grass. She's so done with that stuff.

Wallop

Hammer It Home!

Origin: Wallop is a tinkerer who forged weapons from the bubbling lava pits of Mount Scorch. When he showed his masters how he developed his skills, a fire viper erupted from within the volcano and attacked the village. Wallop used his mammoth hammers to defeat the viper and save his friends. Now he serves as a member of the Skylanders Trap Team.

Personality: Wallop is the hardest-working hero this side of Mount Scorch. His inventive mind is always looking for new things to create.

Most likely to: Use his Traptanium-infused hammers to protect his village and smash bad guys.

Least likely to: Use his Traptanium-infused hammers to smash his village and protect bad guys.

Rock and Roll!

Bop

Origin: Bop grew up wishing he had wings that would help him soar above the clouds. After a little help from his mentor, Bash, Bop studied and trained at Skylanders Academy, learning all about how to be a hero. Now he's living his dream as a member of the Skylanders.

Personality: Bop can be a little headstrong sometimes. But he never gives up, even when the odds are against him. That's the true mark of a hero.

Most likely to: Be a little jealous when his friends go flying.

Least likely to: Glue a pair of wings to his back.

Terrabite

MINI

It's Feeding Time!

Origin: Terrabite learned a lot from his mentor, Terrafin. The most important thing he learned is that a hero doesn't back down from a fight, even when the odds are against him. And now that Terrabite has graduated from Skylanders Academy, he's ready to put his training to the test.

Personality: Terrafin is pretty persistent. If he gets knocked down, he gets right back up again in true hero style.

Most likely to: Challenge bad guys to a boxing match.

Least likely to: Take ballet lessons. It's just not his thing.

Rock and Roll!

Origin: Born without wings, Bash longed to fly. He taught himself how to roll up into a rocky ball and launch himself off cliffs. His revolving talents came in useful when he rescued his dragon brothers from a gang of hunters. He smashed through the hull of the hunter's ship and straight into legend.

Personality: Never tell Bash he can't do something. This resourceful, stubborn Skylander will keep on rolling along until he's proved you wrong.

Most likely to: Get caught moping over his one true love, Flashwing.

Least likely to: Give up without a fight.

Dino-Rang

SKYLANDER

Come *Rang* or Shine!

Origin: A member of a faraway tribe of dinosaur hunters, Dino-Rang was transported to Skylands by a coven of sinister Spell Punks whose Portal magic had gone seriously wrong. Dino-Rang smacked them all the way to the Outlands and then began his quest to find the Twin Diamond Boomerangs. Legend has it that only they have the power to send him home.

Personality: Unlike most disorderly dinosaurs, Dino-Rang is cool and collected. Even though he loves being a Skylander, he still dreams of the hunting plains of his homeland.

Most likely to: Flatten you if you mistake him for a dragon!

Least likely to: Invite a Spell Punk around for a BBQ anytime soon.

Knock Knock . . . Too Late

Origin: Fist Bump was the sleeping protector of the Bubbling Bamboo Forest until the day a swarm of Greebles blasted his home with giant rock-smashing machines! But Fist Bump used his massive stone fists to create an earthquake, destroying the Greebles' machines and driving them away. Terrafin took note and brought Fist Bump to meet Master Eon, where he was welcomed into the Skylanders.

Personality: Fist Bump is always the first person to shake things up at a party. He loves to get loose and rock out.

Most likely to: Sleep on the job. It's okay, though! That's kind of his thing.

Least likely to: Hurt the environment.

Flashwing

Blinded by the Light!

Origin: No one knows where Flashwing comes from. She was spotted crashing to the ground in the heart of a shooting star by Bash. He immediately fell for her beauty, and she immediately blasted him from a cliff using her tail laser. Not quite a romance made in heaven.

Personality: Flashwing knows just how beautiful she appears and also how deadly she can be. She often tries to steal the spotlight from her fellow Skylanders, but her kind heart always shines through in the end.

Most likely to: Boast that she outshines all others.

Least likely to: Admit that she really does like Bash.

The Beam Is Supreme!

Prism Break

Origin: Grumpy rock golem Prism Break didn't mind being trapped in a cave for one hundred years. He'd never liked being around people anyway. But when he was released by a bunch of Mabu miners, he discovered that his arms had been crushed into energy-firing gems.

Personality: While not as cranky as before, Prism Break still prefers his own company, although he's quick to use his precious gem-powered abilities to protect Skylands from attack.

Most likely to: Keep to himself until needed.

Least likely to: Throw a party and invite all his friends.

Rocky Roll

Roll with It!

Origin: Rocky was a digger with a heart of gold, and Roll had dreamed of traveling the globe ever since he was a little pebble. Together they found themselves on the journey of a lifetime, hoping to find the mythical Peek's Peak. What they found instead was friendship. Now together as Rocky Roll, they proudly serve as Skylanders.

Personality: Rocky Roll loves helping people. There isn't anything they wouldn't do for their pals. Their friendship is solid as a rock!

Most likely to: Roll with the punches and crush the competition.

Least likely to: Sit around and wait for destiny to knock on their door.

King of the Sting!

Origin: The Salt Flat Islands' number one Sting Ball player, Scorp saved everyone when an opposing team sneakily used an enchanted water gem to make it rain. The spell went wrong, flooding the islands, but Scorp dived into the depths, retrieved the troublesome gem, and hurled it into the storm clouds.

Personality: Rough-and-tumble Scorp is a real tough guy—but his experience with the gem taught him he could use his amazing abilities for more than just sport.

Most likely to: Take down the opposition—hard!

Least likely to: Lose!

Clobber and Slobber!

Origin: An ancient Earth beast, Slobber Tooth snoozed for thousands of years, until he was awakened by two volcanic islands crashing together. When he rejected Kaos's offer to join his minions, the Portal Master attacked the rest of Slobber's hibernating race—and was clobbered into next week!

Personality: When in doubt, Slobber Tooth will head-butt something. Or tail-thwap it. Or bite it. Or sometimes all three. Ouch!

Most likely to: Butt, thwap, or bite. Haven't you been paying attention?

Least likely to: Sit down and talk things over.

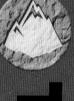

Terrafin

It's Feeding Time!

Origin: Terrafin's time as a Dirt Sea lifeguard came to an end when an explosion turned the sandy oceans into a single sheet of glass. Never one to throw in the towel, Terrafin went on to become a boxing champion and—after being crowned king of the ring—a Skylander beyond compare.

Personality: Nothing gets Terrafin on the ropes. If he's knocked down he gets straight back up again, coming back fighting from any scrap.

Most likely to: Think with his fists. And sometimes also his teeth.

Least likely to: Take it on the chin.

Crusher

GIANTS

s Crush Hour!

Origin: Crusher came from a long line of rock crushers. He traveled all over Skylands to discover the rarest gems and stones that he could crush with his crushing hammer (which, incidentally, is also called Crusher). That was until he heard the Arkeyan King was transforming rocks into weapons, so he decided to crush Arkeyans instead.

Personality: Single-minded and completely unstoppable, Crusher crashes through any situation with the subtlety of a three-ton hammer. He's also incredibly thick-skinned—probably because his skin's made of stone.

Most likely to: Crush things. Hard.

Least likely to: Take up flower-pressing as a hobby.

Another Smash Hit!

SWAP FORCE

Doom Stone

Origin: Originally a statue, Doom Stone was animated by a slobby sorcerer who wanted someone to fetch and carry for him. Happy just to be alive, Doom Stone served his master well, learning the art of Stone Fighting as a hobby—which came in handy when the wizard was kidnapped by his own evil twin!

Personality: This granite gladiator is a fearsome opponent but is always happy to help his friends with any task.

Most likely to: Appear stone-faced in battle.

Least likely to: Stand around. He did enough of that as a statue.

Doom Blade

Stone Fighting meets super skating with this heavyweight SWAP.

Doom Bomb

Rocky top, stinky bottom, full force.

Doom Buckler

The ideal combo for when you want Wash Buckler to join the Column Club.

Doom Charge

Add Tech and Speed abilities to Doom Stone's awesome upper body strength.

Doom Drilla

Earth and Life Elements combine to create a Stone Fighting drilling machine.

Doom Jet

Send Doom Stone skyward to ambush from the air.

Doom Kraken

Make this SWAP for Living Statue and Kraken Up skills together in one powerful package.

Doom Loop

Mix Earth with Magic to create this mystical mash-up.

Doom Ranger

Try this SWAP for a powerful mix of Club Doom and Nova Flash.

Doom Rise

The perfect SWAP to battle and climb your way through Kaos's minions.

Doom Rouser

The ground itself will want to make a run for it when it sees this mighty Earth SWAP.

Doom Shadow

Doom Stone's Living Statue meets Trap Shadow's Dark Magic.

Doom Shake

Take Doom Stone's Stone Fighting prowess to the Land of the Undead.

Doom Shift

Doom Stone gets even closer to doom with Night Shift's ghostly bottom half.

Doom Zone

Doom Stone is now ready for blast off.

Rubble Rouser

Brace f Impac

Origin: For centuries, Rubble Rouser's people dug tunnels by eating their way through rock. Everyone laughed when he first suggested using a drill or hammer instead—until rotten Rock Lords trapped them all deep within Deep Mountain. Rubble Rouser rescued the rock-munchers with a blow from his mighty hammer!

Personality: Rubble Rouser is always looking to improve the way things work—and for new rocks to pulverize with his hammer slam!

Most likely to: Know the drill. And the hammer, for that matter.

Least likely to: Tuck into a salad. Rubble still prefers to snack on stones.

Rubble Blade

Hammer Swing plus speed equals terrified trolls.

Rubble Bomb

Fancy mixing strength with stealth? This could be the SWAP for you.

Rubble Buckler

Sledgehammer body, Octolash tentacles, Skylander supreme!

Rubble Charge

Send Rubble Rouser careering through enemies on Magna Charge's wild wheel.

Rubble Drilla

Double drill it with a Drill Head attack and rotating lower half.

Rubble Jet

Try combining Drill Head and Sky Writing with this slamming SWAP.

Rubble Kraken

Earth meets Fire to create a minion-bashing mega SWAP.

Go the distance for a mighty combo of Gem Quality and Teleport Turbulence.

Rubble Ranger

This Earth-Air SWAP is guaranteed to go down a storm!

Rubble Rise

Climbing ability adds an extra edge to Rubble Rouser's Happy Hammering.

Rubble Shadow

Power meets stealth in this formidable Earth-Magic compound.

Rubble Shake

Take Rubble Rouser on a *ssstampede!*

Rubble Shift

Rock Shards? Check! Luck of the Underbat? Check!

Rubble Stone

Match up a Hammer Swing upper half with a drill-tastic lower half to create this Earth ace.

Rubble Zone

Hammer meets heat in this super SWAP.

Fire

Fire Skylanders

Ka-Boom 61

Wildfire 62

Small Fry 63

Weeruptor 64

Eruptor 65

Flameslinger 66

Fryno 67

Hot Dog 68

Ignitor 69

Smolderdash 70

Sunburn 71

Torch 72

Trail Blazer 73

Hot Head 74

Blast Zone 75

Blast Zone SWAPs 76-79

Fire Kraken 80

Fire Kraken SWAPs 81-84

Boom Time!

Ka-Boom

Origin: Ka-Boom and his clan invented all kinds of gadgets from their home on the ancient volcanic island of Munitions Forge. And when Captain Ironbeard's pirate ships began plundering, Ka-Boom whipped out his greatest weapon ever—the Boom Cannon! He blasted the spiteful scavengers away and soon joined the Skylanders Trap Team.

Personality: Ka-Boom is a thinker and a tinker. He'll mess around with his inventions until he gets them absolutely perfect.

Most likely to: Protect his home at all costs. Because that's what heroes do!

Least likely to: Use his Red Hot Traptanium Cannon to heat up leftovers.

Wildfire

Bringing the Heat

Origin: Wildfire, whose gold color once made him an outcast, is a member of the Fire Claw Clan. After saving a pack of his lion brothers from a flame scorpion, he used his father's enchanted shield to become the mightiest in his clan. Soon Master Eon took notice and made him an official member of the Skylanders Trap Team.

Personality: Wildfire is a loyal lion with a heart of gold, but he can be pretty fierce in battle. He's very protective of the Fire Claw Clan and is always ready to lend them a magical hand when they need it.

Most likely to: Honor his father's legacy by using his Traptanium-bonded shield to fight evil.

Least likely to: Abandon his friends in their time of need.

Crash and Burn!

Origin: Small Fry always tells the truth, even when others don't want to hear it. That's what makes him like his hotheaded mentor, Fryno. Oh, and Small Fry hates it when people lie and cheat! After graduating from Skylanders Academy, he's now matured into his role as a full-fledged Skylander.

Personality: Small Fry has a short temper. It makes him a little hot under the collar.

Most likely to: Tell Fryno when he has a piece of food in his teeth.

Least likely to: Enjoy a nice glass of ice water during a snowstorm.

Born to Burn!

Origin: Everything makes Weeruptor bubble over into a fiery rage. Sometimes it's the little things and sometimes it's the big things. He doesn't just hate evil; he wants to burn it to the ground till there's nothing left but a pile of ashes. That's pretty intense. Good thing Eruptor is around to help keep him in check!

Personality: Weeruptor has a bad temper. Even the slightest thing will make him angry. Sometimes he's just a typical hothead.

Most likely to: Spit a flaming ball of magma at a bad guy.

Least likely to: Relax on an island with his favorite book.

Born to Burn!

Origin: Eruptor was born deep beneath an ancient volcano, a member of a race of hotheaded fire beasts. No one even knew they existed until an argument at a lava-pool party boiled over, causing the volcano to erupt and spew them into the air.

Personality: A flaming force of nature, Eruptor still blows his top from time to time. He doesn't suffer fools gladly, but he tries to keep his fiery temper in check.

Weapon: Eruptor lobs blobs of molten rock and spits out blistering magma balls. When really mad, he's been known to burst into a boiling pool of bubbling plasma.

Most likely to: Turn up the heat on his enemies.

Least likely to: Take a deep breath and keep cool.

Flameslinger

Let the Flames Begin!

Origin: After rescuing a drowning fire spirit, Flameslinger was rewarded with flaming boots that allow him to run at blistering speeds and a magical flaming bow that never misses. After causing a stir by winning every archery contest in Skylands, the universe's hottest bowman was invited to become a Skylander.

Personality: Yes, he may look like a bit of a show-off by firing his arrows while blindfolded, but a courageous heart burns beneath this cocky athlete's chest.

Most likely to: Get straight to the point—about how talented he is.

Least likely to: Miss the target, no matter how fast it is traveling.

Crash and Burn!

Fryno

Origin: A lifetime member of the Blazing Biker Brigade, Fryno wasn't aware that the rest of his biking buddies were in fact good-for-nothing thieves. When he found out, he battered the burglars, broke up the Brigade, and personally returned the booty.

Personality: Fryno is hot on honesty. In fact, liars and cheats make him flaming mad!

Most likely to: Charge in horn-first.

Least likely to: Handle hot merchandise.

Hot Dog

See Spot Burn!

Origin: The Skylanders first met Hog Dog when the molten mutt was spewed up by the Popcorn Volcano. The pup burnt Gill Grunt's tent to the ground, but redeemed himself by saving the group from a lava golem. Having become attached to him, the Skylanders brought him back to Eon's Citadel, where he was quickly made a permanent member of the team.

Personality: Any Skylander's best friend, Hot Dog is exceptionally loyal and is always bounding around like an excitable puppy—which is exactly what he is.

Most likely to: Bury anything he can get his flaming paws on, from Eon's staff to Fright Rider's skeletal steed.

Least likely to: Go hungry. Hot Dog's always on the lookout for a sizzling snack.

Ignitor

Slash and Burn!

Origin: While still in training to be a knight, young Ignatius was sent to slay a dragon. Quaking in his ill-fitting boots, he was tricked by a witch into donning a suit of cursed armor that transformed him into a blazing fire spirit for all time.

Personality: Gallant and trustworthy, Ignatius changed his name to Ignitor and remains true to his pledge to use his powers to protect the innocent.

Most likely to: Launch himself into a heated battle whenever his help is needed.

Least likely to: Join the official Skylands Aren't Evil Witches Brilliant? Society.

Smolderdash

A Blaze of Glory!

Origin: Smolderdash dreamed of being Royal Defender of the Fire Temple, a great honor among her kind. There was just one problem: Her people thought she was cursed, so wouldn't let her anywhere near the place. They soon changed their minds when she rescued the temple's sacred flame from a thieving Kaos.

Personality: As steely and determined as they come, Smolderdash's other dream was to become a Skylander—and now, of course, that dream is a reality!

Most likely to: Whip enemies into shape.

Least likely to: Take no for an answer!

Roast-n-Toast!

Origin: From the moment he hatched in the middle of a volcano, Sunburn was hunted by wizards and witches who wanted to use his half-dragon, half-phoenix feathers in their teleportation spells. After he heard of his amazing abilities, Master Eon offered the flaming hybrid the ultimate protection by making him a Skylander.

Personality: Prankster Sunburn uses his powers of teleportation to play practical jokes on his Skylander buddies, appearing when they least expect it.

Most likely to: Get his team hot under the collar with his constant mischief-making.

Least likely to: Stay in one place for more than a minute at a time.

Torch

Fire It Up!

Origin: Torch loved helping her grandfather take care of the dragons that protected their village. But then an evil Snow Dragon trapped everyone in a glacier! Using her Firespout Flamethrower, Torch freed her people and saved the village. Sadly her grandfather went missing—but with the help of the Skylanders, she'll never give up the search to find him.

Personality: Torch is pretty fearless. Some might say she's hotheaded.

Most likely to: Show you her grandfather's lucky flaming horseshoe.

Least likely to: Open up a snow-cone stand.

The Mane Event!

Origin: When Trail Blazer came upon the mythical Unicorn trapped in a net, he combined his elemental fire with magical cinnamon from the Unicorn's Churro Horn and saved them both from a pack of attacking Dark Wizards! Such power caught the attention of Master Eon, who drafted Trail Blazer into the Skylanders.

Personality: Trail Blazer can be a little hot-tempered when he sees his friends being treated unfairly.

Most likely to: Use a Unocorn's Churro Horn for good.

Least likely to: Use a Unocorn's Churro Horn for evil.

Hot Head

Hey! I'm on Fire!

Origin: The news that a new magical oil had been discovered spread through Skylands like wildfire. Hot Head was first on the scene and plunged into the black gold for a dip. The result was an explosion that destroyed an island and transformed Hot Head into a being capable of creating eternal infernos.

Personality: Impetuous is a good word to describe Hot Head. He just can't help himself. This Fire Giant is always burning with enthusiasm.

Most likely to: Smother his enemies in blazing blobs of burning oil first—and ask questions second.

Least likely to: Take a deep breath and ponder what's happening.

Blast and Furious

Origin: A member of the Skylands Bomb Squad, Blast Zone was an expert at disarming troll explosives—so the trolls decided to show their annoyance by dropping one hundred grenades down his chimney. Thinking with his stomach, the furnace knight swallowed the bombs and flattened the unwelcome visitors with an explosive belch.

Personality: Fiery, but disarming. Blast Zone always puts the safety of his friends first.

Most likely to: Blow a fuse.

Least likely to: Enjoy a nice, refreshing ice cream.

Blast Blade

Fire and ice really shouldn't work this well together!

Blast Bomb

The bombs from the top are almost as harmful as the whiff from the bottom!

Blast Buckler

Combine Blast Zone's Bomb Throw with Wash Buckler's Somersaulty in this classic swap.

Time to take Blast Zone for a spin!

Send those Flaming Bombs underground with a drill-bit base.

Lob Sticky Bombs while careering through the air as a sky-surfer supreme!

Some like to fight Fire with Fire . . . Blast Kraken prefers to combine them together!

77

Blast Loop

Try matching up Ring of Fire with Loop the Loop in this awesome fusion.

Blast Ranger

Ring Blast top, Wild Tornado bottom. Job done!

Blast Rise

Take Blast Zone on a climbing adventure using Spy Rise's Spyder Climb and Laser Legs.

Blast Rouser

Flame Breath and drills for feet? Good luck, bad guys . . . you'll need it!

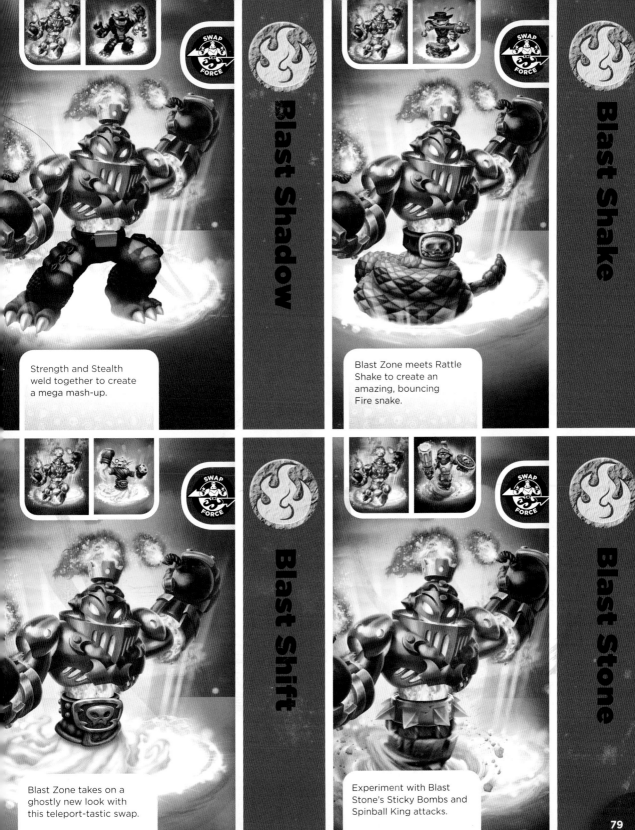

Blast Shadow

Strength and Stealth weld together to create a mega mash-up.

Blast Shake

Blast Zone meets Rattle Shake to create an amazing, bouncing Fire snake.

Blast Shift

Blast Zone takes on a ghostly new look with this teleport-tastic swap.

Blast Stone

Experiment with Blast Stone's Sticky Bombs and Spinball King attacks.

Fire Kraken

Burn to be Wild!

Origin: Skylands' fiery seas are fuelled by the fabled Burning Heart crystal—which is why a fleet of pyromaniac fire trolls wanted to steal it! Fire Kraken, a hot-footed hunter from a tribe of flaming fighters, used his magical staff to set the entire troll armada alight.

Personality: A desire to help others burns in the heart of this young warrior, which is why he left his home to join the Skylanders.

Most likely to: Play with fire.

Least likely to: Get burned out.

Fire Blade

Fire Kraken skates into action with newfound speed!

Fire Bomb

Sparkling Strikes and Sporting Stripes? It can only be Fire Bomb.

Fire Buckler

Fire meets Water as Fire Kraken assumes some familiar-looking tentacles.

Fire Charge

Go for a whirl with Magna Charge's Rad Wheels and Fire Kraken's Glow Stick (not to mention his toothy grin).

Fire Drilla

Dragon Candles up top. Nature's Bounty down below. Fire Drilla has arrived!

Fire Jet

Take Fire Kraken's Dragon Parade into the sky, Boom Jet-style.

Fire Loop

Have a go at mixing Fire Kraken's Glow Stick attack with Hoot Loop's Temporal Whack.

Fire Ranger

Chicken legs, fiery face. It shouldn't work, but it does. Go Fire Ranger!

Fire Rise

Fire, Tech, and Climb all in one Skylander. Fire Rise is tough to beat.

Fire Rouser

Fire Kraken tries some drill shoes on for size . . . and finds they're a perfect fit!

Fire Shadow

Add an extra-large helping of Stealth to Fire Kraken's Sparkling Strikes.

83

Fire Shift

It's Bounce time for everyone's favorite red-hot dragon.

When Fire Kraken needs some help from a Batty Coach, this swap makes perfect sense.

Fire Zone

Take Doom Stone's spinning skills and throw in one burning dragon. Result: scattering minions!

All enemies would be well advised to never enter the Fire Zone!

Life

Life Skylanders

Bushwhack 87

Tuff Luck 88

Barkley... 89

Whisper Elf 90

Bumble Blast... 91

Camo 92

Food Fight... 93

High Five... 94

Shroomboom... 95

Stealth Elf... 96

Stump Smash 97

Zook 98

Zoo Lou 99

Tree Rex 100

Grilla Drilla.. 101

Grilla Drilla SWAPs..102-105

Stink Bomb.. 106

Stink Bomb SWAPs..107-110

Axe to the Max!

Bushwhack

Origin: As a tiny little tree elf in the Arcadian Timberland, Bushwhack studied hard to be a ranger under the guidance of Arbo the tree spirit. When a legion of Lumberjack Trolls attacked, Bushwhack used his knowledge as well as his enchanted axe to drive the trolls away and save the village. Now he's a valued member of the Skylanders Trap Team.

Personality: Bushwhack has a warrior's heart in a tiny elf body. Size doesn't matter when it comes to his passion for heroism.

Most likely to: Use his Traptanium Axe to chop up evil into tiny little bits.

Least likely to: Build a treehouse for a family of trolls.

Tuff Luck

It's Your Lucky Day!

Origin: Hidden within the Random Canyons is Fortunata Springs, the source of good luck throughout Skylands. Tuff Luck and her tribe defended the springs against Kaos and his evil sponge-tankers. With her amazing skills and a little bit of good fortune, Tuff Luck defeated the forces of Kaos and soon joined the Skylanders.

Personality: Tuff Luck has a lot of good stuff going for her. When you drink from the Fortunata Springs, everything kind of works out in your favor.

Most likely to: Use her Traptanium Warblades to slice through evil.

Least likely to: Play it safe. Tuff Luck is all about taking chances.

Barkley

Be Afraid of the Bark!

Origin: Barkley loves and respects nature almost as much as his mentor, Tree Rex. Together they help keep the Arkeyans from polluting everything. Barkley learned all about the forest's magical properties when he attended Skylanders Academy and now he fights to protect the woodlands as a Skylander.

Personality: Barkley will do anything to protect Skylands from dark magic. Mess with him and you'll be barking up the wrong tree!

Most likely to: Tell you all about photosynthesis.

Least likely to: Dump his trash in the forest. That's seriously uncool.

Whisper Elf

MINI

Silent But Deadly!

Origin: Whisper Elf is a little ninja who knows her way around an enchanted forest or two. She learned all kinds of cool ninja skills from her mentor, Stealth Elf. Master Eon saw Whisper Elf's potential when she attended Skylanders Academy and quickly asked her to join the Skylanders after graduation.

Personality: Whisper Elf will always tell you how she's feeling. That can be really awkward sometimes.

Most likely to: Guard the forest with her life!

Least likely to: Throw garbage into a bush. No one likes a litterer.

Bumble Blast

The Perfect Swarm!

Origin: When Kaos heard about the magic honey being produced by the bees of the Radiant Mountains, he sent his minions to swipe the sweet stuff. But his forces of Darkness didn't stand a chance when they came face-to-face with Bumble Blast, the bees' brave living beehive.

Personality: Protective to the extreme, Bumble Blast defends all wildlife, not just his beloved bees. There's nothing sweet about his Honey Blast.

Most likely to: Place himself in danger to defend others.

Least likely to: Tell someone in trouble to buzz off!

Camo

Fruit Punch!

Origin: Half dragon and half plant, Camo was born in the roots of the great Tree of Life. He discovered from an early age that he can make fruit and vegetables grow to huge proportions. Unfortunately, the gigantic greens also tend to blow up, as Eon discovered when he bent over to pick one of Camo's juicy melons.

Personality: Like most dragons, Camo loves a laugh and regularly hides apple and pear grenades in Hugo's fruit bowls, snickering as the Mabu gets smothered in pulp. Heh!

Most likely to: Be found tending to Eon's vegetable plot while not protecting Skylands.

Least likely to: Rest in the shade. This photosynthesizing prankster is a real sun-worshipper.

He Shoots, He Spores!

Shroomboom

Origin: Grown in Kaos's infamous pizza-topping garden, Shroomboom refused to be munched on by the evil Portal Master. The tenacious toadstool led a daring escape over the garden fence, saving his fellow fungi from a plate worse than death.

Personality: Courageous and determined, Shroomboom lets nothing stand in his way. He's always ready to parachute into danger, no matter the risk.

Most likely to: Be the first to jump into battle.

Least likely to: Be seen anywhere near pizza night.

Stealth Elf

Silent But Deadly!

Origin: With no memory of her early years, Stealth Elf was trained by a gnarled old tree-ninja in the heart of an enchanted forest. Before long, the apprentice was more powerful than the shrub-like sensei, so Stealth Elf was sent to Master Eon to complete her Elemental lessons.

Personality: Nature-loving Stealth can sneak into any enemy's territory, but she can also be tactless. She speaks her mind, whether others want to hear it or not.

Most likely to: Tirelessly investigate who she really is and why she can't remember.

Least likely to: Be heard when she sneaks up on you. *Shhh!*

Drop the Hammer!

Stump Smash

Origin: Like his hero, Tree Rex, Stump Smash was content to be a tree, until his forest was logged by a legion of lumberjack trolls. Left with only hammers for hands, Stump Smash took his revenge, reducing the troll's tree-cutting tools to scrap.

Personality: Snappy Stump Smash knows how to bear a grudge. Even after all these years he still seeks out trolls to teach them a lesson. He's no sap.

Most likely to: Pulverize, crush, pound and flatten. And if that doesn't work, cough up a Spiny Acorn.

Least likely to: Ever trust a troll again. Except for Boomer, of course!

ZOOK

Locked and Loaded!

Origin: Most Bambazookers stay stuck in the mud where they sprouted. Not Zook. He was the first of his tribe to venture out in the world, where he immediately used his bamboo bazooka to save a band of elves from a hideous mountain troll.

Personality: Zook is the cheeriest walking bamboo plant you will every meet. He lives life to the fullest and wants to explore every last one of Skylands' many islands.

Most likely to: Have a big grin on his face, even during battle.

Least likely to: Moan and gripe.

Nature Calls!

Zoo Lou

Origin: A powerful shaman, Zoo Lou set out to discover the Seven Strange Strongholds—mystical sites bursting with raw magical power. Studying the ways of the Seven Strange Mages, he returned a master of the natural arts—only to find his homeland overrun by trolls.

Personality: A wild and woolly warrior, Zoo Lou doesn't suffer fools gladly—as the trolls discovered. He summoned every animal on the island to fight the pointy-eared plunderers tooth and claw.

Most likely to: Talk to the animals. And the plants. Sometimes even a pebble or two.

Least likely to: Invite the trolls back for old time's sake.

Tree Rex

Be Afraid of the Bark!

Origin: For centuries, Tree Rex was nothing more than a mighty tree, snoozing peacefully in an ancient woodland. But then magical pollution from a newly built Arkeyan factory destroyed the forest, and mutated him into a vengeful defender of the natural world. BIG mistake, Arkeyans!

Personality: Unwavering in his mission to protect Skylands from evil magic, the very first Skylander is a natural protector who is as wise as he is majestic.

Most likely to: Cast a long shadow over evildoers. Fear the bark!

Least likely to: Put down roots. This titanic tree won't rest until Darkness has passed.

Grilla Drilla

If There's a Drill, There's a Way!

Origin: Every seven years, the Drilla King chooses one of his subterranean subjects to succeed him. During one selection ceremony, the mining monarch was snatched by a bunch of tunneling trolls who wanted the fabled Drilla Diamond. Royal guard Grilla Drilla rescued the king and was named heir to the Drilla Empire.

Personality: Never one to think of himself, Grilla Drilla gave up his jungle throne to become a Skylander—knowing it would mean he could protect even more people!

Most likely to: Go ape. Grilla Drilla goes into a spin if his friends are threatened.

Least likely to: Put himself first.

Grilla Blade

Anyone who thinks monkey-summoning Drillas can't possibly ice-skate should think again!

Grilla Bomb

Life meets Life with this Drilla-Skunk SWAP.

Grilla Buckler

What do you get if you cross an Earth Drilla and a Water Mermasquid? A sea monkey!

Grilla Charge

Give Magna Charge's Rad Wheels some Primate Power.

Grilla Jet

Grilla Drilla's Monkey Call will echo through the skies when he makes this SWAP.

Grilla Kraken

Silverback, red-hot tail. It can only be Grilla Kraken.

Grilla Loop

Looks like it's time for Grilla Drilla to join the Magic circle.

Grilla Ranger

Grilla Drilla's Reaching Mandrill, atop Free Ranger's Wild Tornado. That's SWAP perfection.

Grilla Rise

Unleashing Team Monkey from a Spyder Climb base? That's Grilla Rise!

Grilla Rouser

Grilla Drilla SWAPs drills to take on Rubble Rouser's legs in this Dig-tastic exchange.

Grilla Shadow

Primate Power on top, Shade Steps underneath. What a combo!

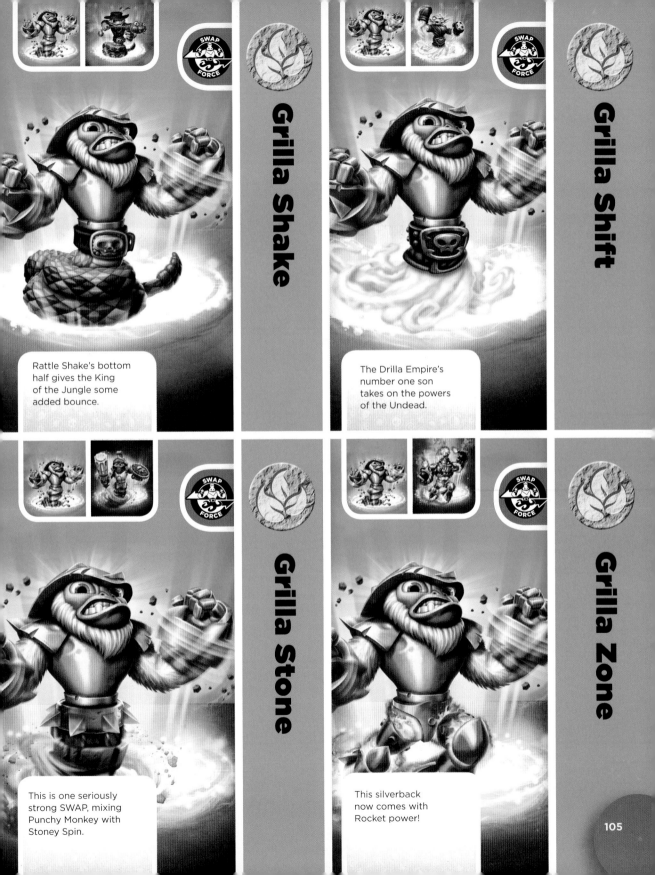

Grilla Shake

Rattle Shake's bottom half gives the King of the Jungle some added bounce.

Grilla Shift

The Drilla Empire's number one son takes on the powers of the Undead.

Grilla Stone

This is one seriously strong SWAP, mixing Punchy Monkey with Stoney Spin.

Grilla Zone

This silverback now comes with Rocket power!

Stink Bomb

Clear the Air!

Origin: Stink Bomb's ninja master believed that only through being surprised could you find yourself. He was constantly jumping out of cupboards, trying to frighten his pupil. One day, Stink Bomb was so shocked he released a pungent pong that caused his master to completely vanish, never to be seen again.

Personality: Resilient Stink Bomb didn't let his master's disappearance put him off. He developed the martial art of Skunk-Fu Fume and wandered Skylands teaching its whiffy ways.

Most likely to: Cause a stink wherever he goes.

Least likely to: Start bottling his revolting stench as a charming line of perfume.

Stink Blade

Stink on ice! It's the ground-breaking show no troll ever wants a ticket for.

Stink Buckler

Enemies are in for serious tentacle trouble when this super SWAP happens.

Stink Charge

Skunk-Fu meets speed to produce one of the most effective mash-ups around.

Stink Drilla

Get ready for drills, thrills, and smells with this Life SWAP.

Stink Jet

Take the Noxious Ninja to the skies, courtesy of Boom Jet's sky-surfer.

Stink Kraken

Stink Bomb's ninja skills get added Bounce from this funky fusion.

Stink Loop

Make this SWAP to try out a mix of Acorn Accuracy and Complete Concentration.

Stink Ranger

Why did the Skunk-Fu chicken cross the road? To unleash stinky ninja terror!

Stink Rise

Stink Bomb's ninja skills plus Spy Rise's Climb abilities make Stink Rise a cracking combo.

Stink Rouser

Life, Earth, and Dig combine . . . it's Stink Rouser!

Stink Shadow

The right SWAP for mixing Stink Bomb's Skunk Eye with Trap Shadow's Bumps in the Night.

109

Stink Shake

A Life skunk meets an Undead snake. Opposites attract!

Stink Shift

This is one Shift you don't want to be on—especially if you're a minion of Kaos!

Stink Stone

Try out Stink Stone's combo of Acorn Accuracy and Jaded Spin.

Stink Zone

Some say Stink Bomb has always had a fiery bottom—but never like this!

Magic

Blastermind 113

Enigma 114

Mini Jini..115

Spry 116

Cobra Cadabra..117

Déjà Vu 118

Double Trouble.. 119

Dune Bug 120

Pop Fizz 121

Spyro...122

Star Strike 123

Voodood 124

Wrecking Ball 125

Ninjini 126

Hoot Loop 127

Hoot Loop SWAPs.. 128-131

Trap Shadow 132

Trap Shadow SWAPs...133-136

Mind Over Matter!

Origin: Blastermind fell into a cavern filled with glowing Psionic Power Crystals while playing a game of "hide-and-sheep" in the Sardonic Mountains. The exotic gems sensed his worried thoughts and bestowed upon him amazing mental powers that he used to save his friends from an attacking Ham Dragon. Now he uses his Traptanium Psionic Helmet as a member of the Skylanders.

Personality: Blastermind is very attuned to the feelings of others and tries hard to help his friends with their problems whenever he can.

Most likely to: Invite the Ham Dragon over for a rump roast.

Least likely to: Fall asleep on the job. He's got *way* too much on his mind!

Out of Sight!

Origin: Enigma grew up in a realm "between worlds" and shared stories of his home with a great Mabu Mystic. When the Darkness invaded Enigma's home, he used the mysterious Sigil of Mystery to fend off the invasion and seal the doorway between worlds forever. His brave sacrifice earned him a spot on the Skylanders Trap Team.

Personality: Sometimes Enigma can be difficult to figure out. He's kind of like a puzzle.

Most likely to: Use his Traptanium Sigil to protect Skylands from magical madness.

Least likely to: Sit around playing Skystones. He's too busy fighting evil.

Any Last Wishes?

MINI

Origin: Mini Jini might be small, but her ninja genie skills always send her enemies packing! She studied potions and spells under her mentor, Ninjini, during her time at Skylanders Academy. Now that she's a member of the Skylanders, Mini Jini is ready to use her blades to slice through evil.

Personality: Mini Jini always looks on the bright side of life. She believes in the power of positive thinking, and her good energy is infectious.

Most likely to: Think good thoughts and hope everything turns out well.

Least likely to: Put a curse on everyone! She's the nice kind of genie.

MINI

All Fired Up!

Origin: Spry has always looked up to his idol and mentor, Spyro. Magical purple dragons stick together like that! Spry can be a little impulsive from time to time, but that's just because he loves being a hero so much. Now that's he's graduated from Skylanders Academy, it's Spry's time to shine.

Personality: Spry is an eager young dragon who wants to fight evil wherever he can. He's also good at learning things quickly, which is a very important part of teamwork.

Most likely to: Remember everything about Skylands.

Least likely to: Sit at home and watch paint dry.

Charmed and Ready!

Origin: Cobra Cadabra learned the art of magic from an illusionist known as The Great Mabuni. The Mysteriously Mad Magic Masters of Mystery didn't like that at all, so they sent a group of wild hares over to cause them some trouble. Thankfully, Cobra Cadabra used his magic flute to stop the brutish rabbits and save the day!

Personality: Cobra Cadabra is a charmer, all right. He's brave, too! When he plays an enchanted tune, everyone listens.

Most likely to: Learn all kinds of cool disappearing acts from The Great Mabuni.

Least likely to: Give away all his secrets. He's a magician, after all.

Did That Just Happen?

Origin: Déjà Vu is a hardworking inventor who built a machine that could speed up time. When a gang of monstrous sea slugs got wind of her invention, they charged her sanctuary looking to steal it! But Déjà Vu turned the tables on the slugs and set off a device that blasted her with amazing powers. Now she uses her mastery of time as a member of the Skylanders.

Personality: Déjà Vu has one of those personalities that makes you think you might have met her before.

Most likely to: Build a device that can cook a three-minute egg in half the time.

Least likely to: Throw rocks at the Tower of Time. That would be asking for trouble.

Boom
Shock-A-Laka!

Origin: For years, spell-caster Double Trouble searched for the wondrous Whispering Water Lily, a flower said to multiply the strength of any hex. Instead, the bewitched bloom gave the tricky tiki man the ability to create exploding doubles of himself. From that day on, Double Trouble was never alone thanks to his army of clones.

Personality: A loner at heart, Double Trouble discovered the joys of companionship through his clones. Always upbeat, the spirited shaman is a bundle of unearthly Eldritch energy.

Most likely to: Sing a song while zapping minions with his supernatural staff.

Least likely to: Complain that he's lonely!

Dune Bug

SKYLANDER

Can't Beat the Beetle!

Origin: Hailing from a long line of enchanted beetles, Dune Bug once guarded a secret underground Arkeyan ruin. Dune would stay up all night reading his home city's ancient books of spells—until, that is, the despicable Sand Mages of Doom tried to raid the library. But Dune didn't let them bug him—he just blasted them with the magic he'd learned.

Personality: Dune Bug covers all the bases. He not only fought off the mages, but managed to bury the city even deeper underground, out of everyone's reach.

Most likely to: Be caught with his mandibles in a book.

Least likely to: Reveal the location of his ancestral home. Even to Eon!

Pop Fizz

The Motion of the Potion!

Origin: Pop Fizz's origins are a mystery—even to himself. Thanks to years of experimenting with his weird and wonderful potions, the addled alchemist doesn't even remember what he originally looked like. His favorite brew is the special soda that transforms him into a snarling berserker beast. Grrr!

Personality: The Skylander who puts the *mad* in *mad scientist*, Pop Fizz is bubbling over with crazy amounts of enthusiasm. And that's before he's glugged from his bonkers beast beaker!

Most likely to: Keep experimenting until he's perfected the perfect potion.

Least likely to: Decide that he likes himself just the way he is.

Spyro

All Fired Up!

Origin: The Scrolls of the Ancients mention a brave purple dragon who started fighting evil almost from the moment he hatched from his egg. No wonder Master Eon traveled to the far and distant dragon realm to invite Spyro to be one of his first Skylanders.

Personality: Headstrong and eager to jump into action, brave Spyro soon learned the benefits of working with a team. Over time, he developed into a natural leader and Eon's right-hand dragon.

Most likely to: Scorch followers of Darkness with his fiery breath.

Least likely to: Forget anything. Spyro has a photographic memory.

Shoot for the Stars!

Origin: Discovering the perfect banishment spell in a rare and dusty scroll, Kaos attempted to make the Skylanders disappear forever. Fortunately for Skylands, the dust got up the Portal Master's nose and he sneezed midspell. Unfortunately for Star Strike, she was dragged from her home halfway across the cosmos by the botched incantation.

Personality: You can't pull the wool over this bewitching alien's massive eyes. Kaos tried to recruit her to his cause—so she zapped him with her magical cosmic powers. Ha!

Most likely to: Send evil into orbit with her Star Fall Blast. It's out of this world.

Least likely to: Attempt to get home. She's a massive fan of Skylands.

Axe First, Questions Later!

Origin: Appointed chief of the Ooga Orcs after braving the terrifying Cave of Trials and recovering the legendary Axe Reaver, Voodood led his tribe into battle against the Darkness. The sole survivor of the calamitous conflict then threw in his lot with the Skylanders, and vowed to take his revenge.

Personality: Determined Voodood will never give up—even if the odds are as grim as his dragon-skull helmet. He will fight until the very end (probably even a little longer, in fact).

Most likely to: Protect his friends and allies, no matter what.

Least likely to: Give up and head home for a sit down and a nice cup of tea.

Wreck-n-Roll!

Origin: Destined to be part of a ravenous wizard's lunch, Wrecking Ball was thrown into a bubbling cauldron. Imagine the mage's shock when the greedy grub guzzled down the entire enchanted stew and grew to twenty times his original size. The mutated maggot even tried to wolf down the warlock—but didn't like the taste of the wizard's beard, so spat him out.

Personality: Possibly the most reckless of all the Skylanders, Wrecking Ball rolls into danger without thought for his own personal safety. The lively larva smashes anything in his path (often) by accident, and is always hungry—even when he's just eaten!

Most likely to: Eat. Just don't stand downwind when he lets out a Power Belch. Yuck.

Least likely to: Skip lunch. Or any meal, for that matter.

Any Last Wishes?

Origin: Trapped within a bewitched bottle for centuries, mystical ninja Ninjini used her time wisely, practicing dual sword techniques within her enchanted prison. Eventually, through sheer force of will, she became strong enough to smash free.

Personality: This genie's magical bottle is always half-full. An eternal optimist, Ninjini spins into battle, convinced she will always succeed, no matter what.

Most likely to: Spend every spare moment polishing her battle skills and spells.

Least likely to: Bottle up her problems.

Origin: Raised by a guild of traveling magicians in Skylands' most renowned circus, Hoot Loop was soon outperforming his conjuring coaches. Pulling Chompies out of hats? Simple. Sawing Rotting Robbies in half? No problem. No trick was too tricky—including teleportation.

Personality: A natural showman, the Amazing Hoot Loop (as he was known) saved the circus from a band of Greebles disguised as sinister clowns, but still found time to take a bow.

Most likely to: Keep practicing. Hoot Loop is determined to learn every spell ever created.

Least likely to: Be modest. Hoot Loop is the first to boast about his extraordinary abilities.

Hoot Blade

Hoot Loop on Freeze Blade's ice skates? Owl's about that then!

The feathery magician kicks up a real stink when this ace SWAP happens.

Hoot Buckler

Feathers and tentacles—rarely seen, always mean.

Hoot Loop fuses with Magna Charge to gain some incredible speed.

This Magic-Life combo adds a Dream Beam to Coconut Mayhem.

Hoot Loop wasn't born to fly—but sure looks the part on Boom Jet's sky-surfing legs.

Expect some slightly singed feathers from this Magic-Fire fusion.

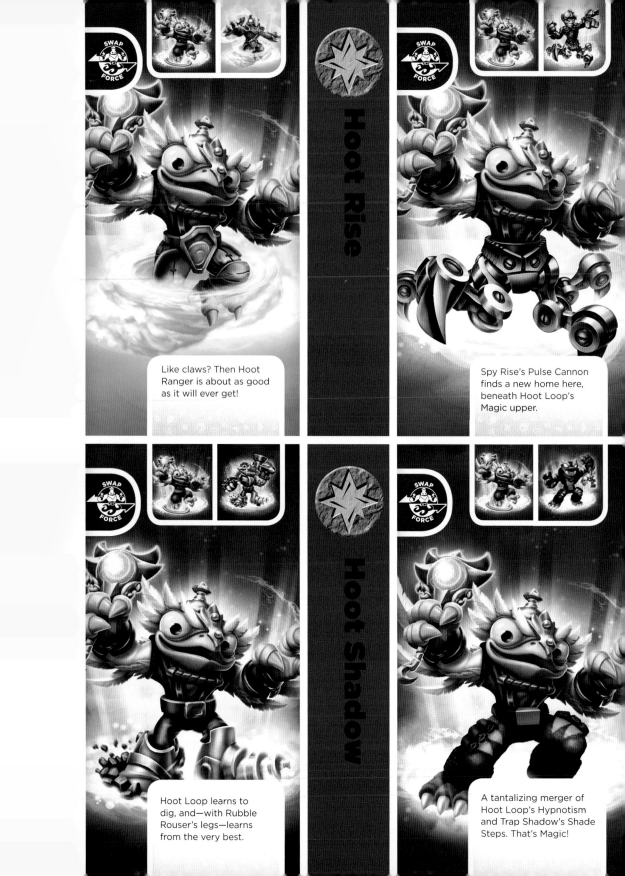

Hoot Rise

Like claws? Then Hoot Ranger is about as good as it will ever get!

Spy Rise's Pulse Cannon finds a new home here, beneath Hoot Loop's Magic upper.

Hoot Shadow

Hoot Loop learns to dig, and—with Rubble Rouser's legs—learns from the very best.

A tantalizing merger of Hoot Loop's Hypnotism and Trap Shadow's Shade Steps. That's Magic!

Hoot Shake

A great combo for adding Rattle Shake's Graveyard Smash to Hoot Loop's Mass Hypnosis.

Hoot Shift

Sorcerer meets phantom-weight champion in this tough-to-beat combo.

Hoot Stone

Send Hoot Loop into a Stoney Spin using Doom Stone's rock-hard base.

Hoot Zone

Try out Hoot Loop's Deep Asleep alongside Blast Zone's Tempered Fire.

131

Trap Shadow

SWAP FORCE

Hide and Sleek!

Origin: The finest feline tracker in his tribe, Trap Shadow was the go-to cat if you wanted something caught—which is why a cabal of sinister sorcerers decided to seize the hirsute hunter. They wanted him to help them capture the only being powerful enough to stop their evil plots—Master Eon!

Personality: You have to get up early to catch Trap Shadow out—as the wicked wizards discovered. He sniffed out their plans and trapped them before they could trap him (or Eon, for that matter).

Most likely to: Keep himself to himself. However, since becoming a Skylander he's been trying to become a team player.

Least likely to: Forget where he left something.

Trap Blade

Skylands' top trapper takes to the ice with this Magic-Water combo.

Trap Bomb

A great SWAP for fans of Stealth, mixing Trap Shadow's cunning with Stink Bomb's martial arts know-how.

Trap Buckler

Add Wash Buckler's Ink Trail to Trap Shadow's Sharp Magic. SWAP supreme!

133

Trap Drilla

Put Trap Shadow on Magna Charge's wheel for the perfect blend of speed and smarts.

Grilla Drilla's Planted Turret base adds some Dig power to the Nocturnal Predator.

Trap Kraken

Gloom and Boom, and Boom again!

Fire Kraken's Bounce and Trap Shadow's Snap Trap combine to form one ace adventurer.

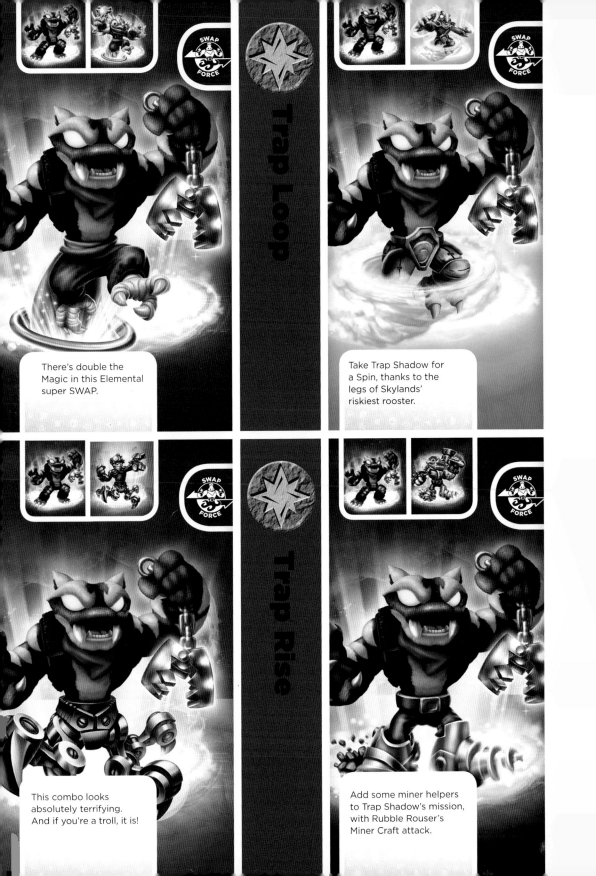

Trap Loop

There's double the Magic in this Elemental super SWAP.

Take Trap Shadow for a Spin, thanks to the legs of Skylands' riskiest rooster.

Trap Rise

This combo looks absolutely terrifying. And if you're a troll, it is!

Add some miner helpers to Trap Shadow's mission, with Rubble Rouser's Miner Craft attack.

Trap Shake

Snap Trap and Goliath Bone Snake in one Skylander? It's got to be seen to be believed.

Trap Shift

This Nocturnal Predator is also a teleporting ghoul.

Trap Stone

Add Stone Fighting to Trap Shadow's bulging skill set.

Trap Zone

Now Trap Shadow is too hot to handle!

Tech

Tech Skylanders

Gear Shift 139

Jawbreaker 140

Drobit 141

Trigger Snappy 142

Boomer 143

Chopper 144

Countdown...145

Drill Sergeant..146

Drobot..147

Sprocket 148

Tread Head..149

Trigger Happy 150

Wind-Up 151

Bouncer 152

Magna Charge 153

Magna Charge SWAPs.................................154-157

Spy Rise 158

Spy Rise SWAPs 159-162

All Geared Up!

Gear Shift

TRAP MASTER

Origin: King Mercurus created Gear Shift on the Tech island of Metallana so he'd have a robot daughter to keep him company. But Gear Shift wasn't into royal stuff and wanted to be a hero to her people instead. When some Undead Stormriders attacked, she led the change against them and saved the day. Soon after, Master Eon gifted her some Traptanium-forged gear and welcomed her as a new member of the Skylanders Trap Team.

Personality: Gear Shift's passion and spirit are an inspiration to her teammates. She's also quick on her feet.

Most likely to: Outsmart her enemies and use her abilities to help people.

Least likely to: Use her Great Gear to cook dinner for Undead Stormriders.

Jawbreaker

TRAP MASTER

Down for the Count!

Origin: Jawbreaker and his robot friends lived deep underground in a world of machines. It was their job to protect the Sky Train, which transported them across a thousand different islands every day. An army of Gear Trolls invaded, hoping to take over the Sky Train, but Jawbreaker used his enormous fists to hand them a crushing defeat. His bravery earned him a place in the Skylanders.

Personality: Jawbreaker likes being an individual, even though his robot pals think he should be more like them. Sometimes you've just got to dare to be different.

Most likely to: Use his Traptanium fists to squash bad guys and lead the Trap Team to victory!

Least likely to: Do what everyone else is doing.

Blink and Destroy!

MINI

Drobit

Origin: Never mess with a dragon in a robot suit, especially one that's a supergenius like Drobit! He may be small, but his mentor, Drobot, always made him feel like he was in the big time. Now that he's graduated from Skylanders Academy, Drobit is ready to show his fellow Skylanders that he's ready for action.

Personality: Drobit enjoys studying and is known to be a smarty-pants. He's got a big heart, too, which is a nice balance.

Most likely to: Get his entire list of chores done before the sun is up!

Least likely to: Give up. Heroes *never* give up!

MINI

Trigger Snappy

No Gold, No Glory!

Origin: Trigger Snappy is an eager little bandit who takes after his mentor, Trigger Happy. When trouble blows into town, these two gremlins blow it right back out. Trigger Snappy graduated proudly from Skylanders Academy even though it felt like it took him *forever* to do it. He can be pretty antsy sometimes.

Personality: Trigger Snappy is a ball of positive energy. He's funny and happy, and his teammates love being around him. That must be nice.

Most likely to: Stay at target practice all day long.

Least likely to: Daydream. He's too anxious!

Bring the Boom!

Boomer

Origin: Like all trolls, Boomer likes blowing things up. Unlike other trolls, he doesn't like waging war. The explosive-loving tyke turned his back on the troll army after saving an entire town from being destroyed by his battalion. He later became the first (and only) troll ever to be made a Skylander.

Personality: Explosive! Overenthusiastic Boomer is bursting with manic energy, but is kind through and through. No wonder his troll mother never understood him.

Most likely to: Blow things up, be they enemies, buildings, or sheep. Actually, especially if they're sheep.

Least likely to: Want everyone to keep the noise down. *Shhh!*

Chopper

Dino Might!

Origin: Chopper built a Gyro-Dino-Exo-Suit so he could enter a hunting competition honoring his village idol, Roarke Tunga. But when a volcano eruption threatened the village, Chopper jumped into action, using his suit to get everyone to safety. Master Eon saw that good things come in small packages and soon offered Chopper a place with the Skylanders.

Personality: Chopper might be a little guy, but he's got big ideas. His passion and bravery always impress his teammates.

Most likely to: Drop everything he's doing to help his friends.

Least likely to: Bite your head off. He's not that kind of dinosaur.

Countdown

I'm the Bomb!

Origin: Discovered trapped in a block of ice by a team of snowboarding yetis, Countdown was taken home and defrosted. There was only one problem—the living bomb had no memories of life before he was frozen. Bogus!

Personality: Countdown blows up at a moment's notice, although there is one drawback. Every time he explodes, he loses his memory all over again. Why? He can't remember.

Most likely to: Explode, obviously.

Least likely to: Remember that he's just exploded!

Drill Sergeant

Licensed to Drill!

Origin: Buried beneath the ground for 10,000 years, Arkeyan bulldozer Drill Sergeant was reactivated after being accidentally discovered by Terrafin. Initially confused by his Arkeyan-free existence, Drill Sergeant threw his lot in with the Skylanders and found a new purpose in life.

Personality: Built to obey orders (as well as plow his way through mountainsides), Drill Sergeant follows rules to the letter, never wavering until the job is done.

Most likely to: Blast and bore his way through any obstacle.

Least likely to: Disobey his Portal Master. Drill Sergeant is a stickler for the chain of command.

Blink and Destroy!

Drobot

Origin: Never the strongest flyer, young Drobot was blown off course and crashed into a secret Arkeyan tech stash. Using the gadgetry he discovered, this smart dragon constructed a robotic flying suit and, armed to the cybernetic teeth, joined the Skylanders.

Personality: A super genius, Drobot analyzes everything he comes across. While he seemed cold and calculating at first, the Skylanders soon discovered that he is as brave as he is intelligent.

Most likely to: Solve thirteen problems, retune his Galvanized Bladegears, and zap an army of trolls with his eye lasers, all before breakfast.

Least likely to: Say, "Sorry, I don't understand."

Sprocket

The Fix Is In!

Origin: Born to wealthy Golding parents, Sprocket spent all her time with her gizmo-loving uncle. When Kaos nabbed him to build weapons of war, Sprocket constructed a fully operational battle suit (complete with patented Gun-O-Matic assault turrets) and rushed off to rescue him.

Personality: Resourceful Sprocket isn't one to sit back and let others do the work. She jumps in with both armored feet, creating solutions for every problem imaginable.

Most likely to: Strip a machine and rebuild it in seconds to see how it works.

Least likely to: Stop tinkering.

Tread and Shred!

Origin: Tread Head was a lonely orphan in the Dizzying Dunes. He scavenged for parts and soon built a crude motorbike that he hoped would win a local race. His opponents made fun of him, but they stopped laughing when Tread Head saved them all from a bunch of goblins! He lost the race, but he'd soon win a place among the Skylanders.

Personality: Tread Head prefers substance over style. It's what's inside that matters the most. The outside is just for show.

Most likely to: Save his enemies even when they're being rude. What a guy!

Least likely to: Let a bunch of nasty goblins get his bike dirty.

SKYLANDER

Trigger Happy

No Gold, No Glory!

Origin: Golden guns blazing, Trigger Happy first appeared on the scene when he rode a band of bank-robbing bandits out of a distant frontier town. The townsfolk became rich on the stumpy stranger's bullion bullets, and Trigger Happy became the most famous goldslinger in Skylands.

Personality: Trigger Happy by name, Trigger Happy by nature. This giggling gremlin never stops firing his guns and cackling like a lunatic. According to rumor, he even snickers in his sleep.

Most likely to: Shoot anything that moves (and quite a lot of things that don't).

Least likely to: Put down his guns (unless it's in order to pick up some even bigger ones).

All Wound Up!

Origin: Created by a time-obsessed toymaker, Wind-Up helped his master wind his extensive clock collection. But when the toymaker was accidentally ripped out of time and space, Wind-Up found himself defending the temporal toyroom from cylopses with an eye for time travel.

Personality: Wind-Up is always on time. Bursting with coiled-up energy, he's also always ready to spring into action.

Most likely to: Get his cogs in a spin if plans don't run like clockwork.

Least likely to: Be late for anything!

Bouncer

Deal with the Wheel!

Origin: Once an All-Star Roboto Ball player, Bouncer was press-ganged into guarding a Mabu mine by the evil Arkeyans. Touched by the prisoners' continued devotion to him, Bouncer freed them and joined the Skylanders to defeat the Arkeyan threat.

Personality: A robot Giant with a huge personality, Bouncer always plays to the crowd. Forever the showman, Bouncer is exceptionally loyal to his fans but despises cheaters.

Most likely to: Unleash a ricocheting bouncy ball. Those fingers are loaded!

Least likely to: Fade into the background. Bouncer loves the limelight!

Magna Charge

Attract to Attack!

Origin: Magna Charge always wanted to be accepted by his fellow mighty Ultron robots, but there was one problem— his head was a giant magnet. He couldn't walk down the street without other robots being dragged toward him. So poor Magna was banished to a distant island, where he learned how to master his mysterious magnetic power.

Personality: Magnetic! Get it? No? Oh, forget it.

Most likely to: Wonder what happened to the rest of his people. When he returned to the Ultron base, he discovered that everything had been destroyed.

Least likely to: Push people away. Magna's speedster antics always attract a crowd.

Magna Blade

Freeze Blade's super-fast ice skates take on their own Magnetic Personality.

Magna Bomb

Magna Bomb mixes the Plasma Shots of an Ultron Robot with the Sneaky Tactics of a Skunk-Fu ace.

Magna Buckler

Take Magna Charge for a Climb on Wash Buckler's Sea Legs.

Magna Drilla

Drill down to the heart of the battle with this ground-shattering combo.

Magna Jet

Magna Charge on Boom Jet's Gun Ship? A match made in Skylands!

Magna Kraken

Take that Heavy Blaster, and go for a bounce!

Magna Loop

Tech and Magic combine here like only a one-eyed magnet and an enchanted owl can.

155

Magna Ranger

This robot chicken has Wind Powered drumsticks!

Magna Rise

It's Tech time with this Spyder Climb switch.

Magna Rouser

The Ultron Robot gains Earthy Fortitude.

Magna Shadow

Take Magna Charge for a Prowl on Trap Shadow's sturdy legs.

Magna Shake

Give Magna Charge a spring in his step. (Or should that be slither?)

Magna Shift

Magna Charge gains the power to suck enemies into a Vortex of Doom.

Magna Stone

Like a Speedy Spinner? Magna Stone will be right up your street!

Magna Zone

A terrific twosome of Magnetic Buildup and Armor Plating.

It's Classified!

Origin: The son of Skylands' top private investigator, Spy Rise faced the biggest mystery of his life when his dad disappeared. Following a lengthy search, the spiderlike robot finally scuttled his way to where his pa was being held prisoner by a group of villains wanting to control Mount Cloudbreak, a magical volcano.

Personality: Spy Rise never gives up. The persistent P.I. sticks with a job until everything's wrapped up.

Most likely to: Keep a secret. This is one trustworthy Tech-head.

Least likely to: Weave a web of lies. Spy Rise is as honest as they come.

Spy Blade

The private investigator switches his spider legs for super skates.

Spy Bomb

That stink probably won't help with going undercover—but it sure drives enemies away!

Spy Bucker

Tech meets Water to create this hardy hero.

Spy Charge

Spy Rise takes on a speedy new approach.

Spy Drilla

Here's a combo and a half: Spyder Sting up above, Coconut Mayhem down below.

Spy Jet

Spy Rise gets Rocket Fuel!

Spy Kraken

Spy Rise: now with added bounce!

Spy Loop

What do you get if you cross a Tech Spyder and a Magic owl? One sensational Skylander.

Spy Ranger

A potent mix of Electroweb Pulse Bomb and Tornado Vacuum Boost.

Spy Rouser

With those ace drilling boots, no wonder Spy Rouser always looks so pleased with himself.

Spy Shadow

Tracking plus trapping makes Spy Shadow one of the sneakiest SWAPs around.

161

Spy Shake

Step one: remove Spyder legs. Step two: replace with snake tail. Step three: defeat Kaos!

Spy Shift

Take Spy Rise Close to Doom with Night Shift's spooky lower half.

Spy Stone

How about mashing up Experimental Webs with Belt Pelters? Done!

Spy Zone

Things really start to heat up when Spy Rise takes on these red-hot rockets.

Undead

Undead Skylanders

Krypt King 165

Short Cut 166

Eye-Small 167

Hijinx 168

Bat Spin 169

Chop Chop 170

Cynder 171

Fright Rider 172

Funny Bone 173

Ghost Roaster 174

Grim Creeper 175

Hex 176

Roller Brawl 177

Eye-Brawl 178

Night Shift 179

Night Shift SWAPs 180-183

Rattle Shake 184

Rattle Shake SWAPs 185-188

I've Got the Edge!

Krypt King

Origin: Krypt King is a ghostly knight who once roamed Skylands searching for adventure. His travels brought him to an ancient Arkeyan weapon vault, where he found a powerful suit of armor and claimed it for himself. After defeating a battalion of war machines, Krypt King put his heroic abilities to good use by becoming a member of the Skylanders Trap Team.

Personality: Krypt King may look imposing, but he's really just a curious spirit who's looking to settle down with the right suit of armor.

Most likely to: Use a humongous Traptanium sword to chop his mechanical enemies into pieces.

Least likely to: Use a humongous Traptanium sword to chop up a bunch of vegetables to make a salad.

Short Cut

Cut to the Chase!

Origin: Short Cut and his magic scissors created the most beautiful clothes in all of Skylands. But when an armada of Skeleton Pirates stormed in, Short Cut sewed their pants together while they were sleeping and saved the day. That's what they get for trying to force him to make a magic hat with special powers!

Personality: Short Cut can be a perfectionist, but only because he loves what he does. He puts a lot of time and energy into creating each masterpiece.

Most likely to: Use his Traptanium Shears to cut through the competition.

Least likely to: Steal golden yarn from a fortune-teller. That's not a nice thing to do.

I've Got My Eye on You!

MINI

Eye-Small

Origin: Eye-Small may look like a cute little cyclops, but he'll jump into a fight at the bat of an eye. He's a scrapper like that. Eye-Small learned how to be a hero from his mentor, Eye-Brawl. Now that Eye-Small has graduated from Skylanders Academy, he's looking toward a bright future with the Skylanders.

Personality: Eye-Small pays keen attention to detail. He notices just about everything. He is an eyeball, after all.

Most likely to: Challenge his friends to a staring contest.

Least likely to: Back down from a challenge.

Hijinx

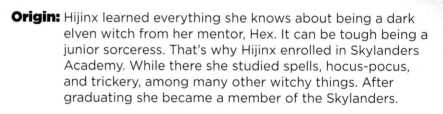

Fear the Dark!

Origin: Hijinx learned everything she knows about being a dark elven witch from her mentor, Hex. It can be tough being a junior sorceress. That's why Hijinx enrolled in Skylanders Academy. While there she studied spells, hocus-pocus, and trickery, among many other witchy things. After graduating she became a member of the Skylanders.

Personality: Hijinx has a reputation for being too serious and maybe a little creepy. But that's okay. She's too focused on her work to notice.

Most likely to: Recite a spell that will rain skulls down upon her enemies.

Least likely to: Tell a joke. Her sense of humor is really weird.

Bat Spin

No Rest for the Wicked!

Origin: After being separated from her underground home as a child, Bat Spin was adopted by a colony of magical bats. The bats raised her as one of their own until a band of Undead Trolls invaded the colony. Bat Spin quickly stopped the Trolls from destroying her people and was rewarded with a membership in the Skylanders.

Personality: Bat Spin was born in the underworld, which makes her witchy in a good way. She's also pretty cool under pressure and isn't known to fly off the handle.

Most likely to: Hang out with her bat friends.

Least likely to: Attend a Troll birthday party.

Chop Chop

Slice and Dice!

Origin: A member of the elite guard, Chop Chop refused to believe his masters had all fallen when the Arkeyan Empire crumbled. He scoured Skylands for centuries, searching for the last standing Arkeyan officer to provide him with new orders. That is, until he chanced upon Eon and was recruited as a Skylander.

Personality: Make no bones about it, Chop Chop is more than a little scary. But he's also a brave, indomitable spirit who never, ever gives up.

Most likely to: Keep fighting, no matter the odds. This skeleton has guts.

Least likely to: Mope around about the fact he's got no *body* to care about.

Volts and Lightning!

Cynder

Origin: The sinister Dragon King Malefor took Cynder under his evil wing before she had even hatched, and taught her to terrorize the countryside. It took a painful defeat at the hands of Spyro to show Cynder the error of her ways and turn her to the side of good.

Personality: Cynder still has a wicked side, but is trying hard to control her darker impulses. While she is loyal to the Skylanders, she has a sharp tongue and can be spiky when riled.

Most likely to: Shock her enemies with a burst of Spectral Lightning.

Least likely to: Hang out in the sunshine. Cynder still prefers the dark.

Fright Rider

Fear the Spear!

Origin: When Fright Rider was sent to the Land of the Undead by jealous jousting competitors, his nervous ostrich steed Ozzy guzzled a bag of skele-oats, transformed into a flightless skeleton and raced to his friend's aid. The duo returned, jousted to victory, and charged off to join the Skylanders.

Personality: Fright Rider and Ozzy are a gallant and courageous pair, honor-bound to right wrongs wherever they roam.

Most likely to: Lead the attack from the front. *Chaaaaarge!*

Least likely to: Stick their heads in the sand until danger passes.

Funny Bone

I Have a Bone to Pick!

Origin: Funny Bone grew up on Punch Line Island, home to the Eternal Chuckling Trees that magically make everyone laugh. One day the dastardly Count Moneybone invaded, thinking he could use the trees to make a "Funny Bomb" that would keep everyone laughing forever. But Funny Bone defeated the Count, earning him a place with the Skylanders.

Personality: Funny Bone is very protective. He always knows when danger is afoot. How does he know? Well, let's just say he gets a *funny* feeling about it.

Most likely to: Bury his neighbor's birthday cake on a breezeless day. Don't ask.

Least likely to: Watch a really serious movie.

Ghost Roaster

No Chain, No Gain!

Origin: Olav the chef fell off the side of a mountain while searching for wool for his famous sheep-fleece stew. Tumbling into the Valley of the Undead, he was transformed into a bony ghoul with a taste for ghosts. After gobbling up an entire Undead village, the spooks chained the now-renamed Ghost Roaster to a spectral ball of spikes.

Personality: Eternally hungry, cackling Ghost Roaster has promised Eon that he will only snack on evil spirits.

Most likely to: Gorge himself on things that go bump in the night.

Least likely to: Decide to munch on a nice, fresh salad instead.

Grim Creeper

Your Time Is Up!

Origin: Grim Creeper struggled to get a place at the prestigious Grim Acres School for Ghost Wrangling, but everything changed when the faculty was caught in a spook stampede. Grim swept into action, sending the specters screaming with a swipe of his scary scythe.

Personality: He may be grim by name and also nature, but this reaper is passionate about fighting evil and will always be a hero through and through.

Most likely to: Stand his ground whatever the situation.

Least likely to: Take up flower arranging.

Hex

Fear the Dark!

Origin: Said to be the most powerful sorceress in the history of Skylands, Hex found herself hounded by the henchmen of Malefor. She took the battle to the Dragon King, defeating him by means of the dark arts. In the process, she was forever transformed into a ghostly Undead witch.

Personality: Imperious and mysterious, spooky Hex isn't known for cracking smiles. She has cracked a few skulls in her time, though, thanks to her dark bone magic.

Most likely to: Harness the forces of Darkness to strike terror into the hearts of evildoers.

Least likely to: Share a joke. Or even like a joke in the first place, come to think of it.

Roller Brawl

Let's Roll!

Origin: As the top jammer in the Undead Roller Derby League, vampire Roller Brawl picked up an unwanted admirer—Kaos. He declared his undying love, and her overprotective elder brothers declared they would flatten him. That's probably why he had them taken prisoner by Drow!

Personality: Roller Brawl never gives up. Realizing that she was no match for the Drow on her own, she joined the Skylanders to fight lovesick Kaos.

Most likely to: Keep searching for her lost brothers, wherever they are.

Least likely to: Date Kaos. Can you imagine it? Gross!

Eye-Brawl

I've Got My Eye on You!

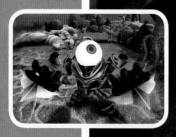

Origin: Centuries ago, a flying eyeball challenged a headless Giant to a staring competition. A fight broke out between the pair and, after a century of relentless scrapping, the duo decided to join forces to form the creepy colossus known as Eye-Brawl.

Personality: Proving that two eerie Undead entities are better than one, Eye-Brawl is big on team work. He's also hyper-observant. Nothing gets past Eye-Brawl (without being thumped, that is!).

Most likely to: Give the forces of Darkness the evil eye.

Least likely to: Roll his eye at you. (Unless you promise to roll it back!)

Roll with the Punches!

Night Shift

Origin: Baron Night Shift had it all—a huge mansion in the Batcrypt Mountains and a massive fortune. However, the batty boxing fan gave it all up to become a prizefighter. He was soon crowned phantom-weight champion, without biting a single opponent. (Okay, there was one . . . but he was asking for it!)

Personality: Night Shift always plays by the rules, so when the Skylands Boxing Federation banned Teleportation he had to give up the sport he loved!

Most likely to: Float like a butterfly, bite like a vampire bat.

Least likely to: Take off his boxing gloves. He even keeps them on in the tub!

Night Blade

When the Undead get ice skates, you know things are getting serious.

Night Bomb

What's worse: a phantom or a phantom smell? Now you can have both!

Night Buckler

While the top half's delivering a One-Two Punch, the bottom half can spurt out an Ink Trail.

Night Charge

Terror on wheels! Night Shift meets Magna Charge.

Night Drilla

One of those things that go thump in the night!

Night Jet

Leave a spectral trail across the sky with this Undead-Air mix.

Night Kraken

It's not often you see Night Shift smile—but this SWAP always gets him Kraken Up.

181

Night Loop

It's Vampire's Bite Time! And Loop the Loop time, for that matter.

Night Ranger

Take Free Ranger from bantamweight to phantom-weight.

Night Rise

Add some Climbing power to Night Shift's prize-winning range of attacks.

Night Rouser

Here's one to try: Pay Day from Night Shift, and Boulder Toss from Rubble Rouser.

Night Shadow

When it's time for a Shadow Kick, there's nowhere more shadowy than the Land of the Undead.

Night Shake

This Undead match-up is the stuff of nightmares . . . troll nightmares!

Night Stone

Make that ghoul Spin Right Around!

Night Zone

Undead meets Fire to form this tough-to-beat terror.

Rattle Shake

Go Ahead Snake My Day!

Origin: Rattle Shake knew the Cloudbreak Islands like the back of his scales, which was why a gang of pesky cowboys threatened to plunder his hometown unless he led them to an enchanted treasure trove inside Mount Cloudbreak. The silly moos didn't bargain on Rattle ssssummoning every sssssnake on the island to ssssend them packing.

Personality: Shake's enemies think he is sinister. In fact, so do some of his friends. But you can be sure that he's no slippery character—Rattle is a virtuous viper.

Most likely to: Get enemies rattled with his Snake Shot catapult.

Least likely to: Hide beneath a rock. This spooky serpent is anything but shy.

Rattle Blade

If there's one thing enemies fear more than a Spring Loaded Snake, it's a Spring Loaded Snake on ice skates.

Rattle Bomb

Think you're scared of snakes? Wait until you've seen one combined with a ninja skunk!

Rattle Buckler

Turn this rattler into a Water snake with Rattle Buckler!

185

Rattle Charge

Extra speed, for extra bite.

Rattle Drilla

Nature's Bounty now comes with added Snake Bite.

Rattle Jet

Armed to the Fangs runs into some serious Turbulence with this top SWAP.

Rattle Kraken

Keep Rattle Shake's Bounce, while adding in a touch of Fire.

Rattle Loop

That hat! That snake! Those Magic talons! It has to be Rattle Loop.

Rattle Ranger

Snake master turns storm chaser with this epic combo.

Rattle Rise

A snake top and a spider's legs? It's Kaos's actual worst nightmare.

Rattle Rouser

Give this a go: Armed to the Fangs plus So Bold. Explosive!

187

Rattle Shadow

Fans of Undead Elemental power and stealth sneakiness will lap this guy up.

Rattle Shift

Undead squared! If you like your SWAPs on the creepy side, it's Rattle Shift for you!

Rattle Stone

Send that snake into a Stoney Spin with Rattle Stone.

Rattle Zone

Step inside the Rattle Zone . . . if you dare!

Water

Lob-Star 191

Snap Shot 192

Gill Runt 193

Thumpling...194

Chill..195

Echo 196

Flip Wreck 197

Gill Grunt 198

Punk Shock 199

Rip Tide... 200

Slam Bam 201

Wham-Shell 202

Zap..203

Thumpback...204

Freeze Blade 205

Freeze Blade SWAPs 206-209

Wash Buckler...210

Wash Buckler SWAPs 211-214

Star Bright, Star Fight!

TRAP MASTER

Origin: Everyone in the kingdom of Star City knew that Lob-Star was the best cook under the sea. But Lob-Star had been studying an ancient and mysterious fighting style, as well. When a gigantic Leviathan overtook the city and threatened the King Fish, Lob-Star used his abilities to drive the monster away. Master Eon took soon took notice and offered him a place with the Skylanders Trap Team.

Personality: Lob-Star is a disciplined crustacean and a hard worker. He's been able to accomplish great things by being patient and understanding in his studies.

Most likely to: Use his Traptanium Throwing Stars to serve his enemies a taste of defeat.

Least likely to: Eat a crab cake. That's like chowing down on your best friend!

Snap Shot

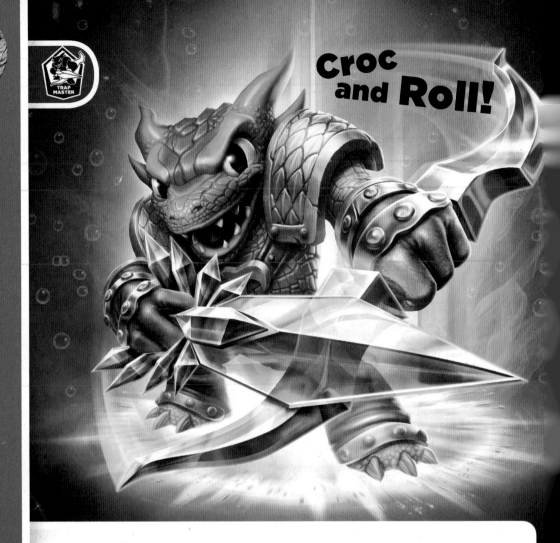

Croc and Roll!

Origin: Hunting for Chompies in Swamplands is pretty easy when you're a scary ole Crocagator like Snap Shot. His nose can sniff out stinky monsters from a mile away. Snap Shot's awesome tracking skills not only earned him membership in the Skylanders but also a leadership position on the Trap Masters team.

Personality: Snap Shot is pretty darn fearless. You might be, too, if you used weapons made of pure Traptanium.

Most likely to: Show his elf pals how to be a master with a bow and arrow.

Least likely to: Cuddle up with a good book and a hot cup of cocoa.

Fear the Fish!

Origin: Gill Runt may be small, but he packs a lot of power! He learned how to be the toughest commando around under the guidance of his mentor, Gill Grunt. His bravery in battle impressed even his colleagues at Skylanders Academy. Now he happily serves as a member of the Skylanders.

Personality: Gill Runt is the best friend anyone could ever have. He's trustworthy and loyal, and he gets the job done. What more can anyone ask for?

Most likely to: Get his friend's back during a fight.

Least likely to: Sing a song. He sounds a little waterlogged.

Thumpling

Hail to the Whale!

Origin: Ever since he was a little whale, Thumpling dreamed of sailing the high seas on a quest for adventure. Oh, and fishing! He dreamed of that, too. Thumpling studied hard at Skylanders Academy and eventually joined his mentor, Thumpback, as a member of the Skylanders. Together they tell evildoers to stuff it in their blowhole!

Personality: Thumpling is a dedicated hero who'll always be there whenever his teammates need him.

Most likely to: Daydream about catching a gigantic fish.

Least likely to: Blow his lid. He's not that kind of whale.

Chill

Stay Cool!

Origin: Once the captain of the Snow Queen's personal guard, Chill was respected throughout the Ice Kingdom. Sadly, her guard dropped when cyclops hordes swept across the northern realms and took their frosty ruler prisoner. Feeling disgraced, Chill set out on a quest to save the Queen, becoming a Skylander on her journey.

Personality: Noble and proud, Chill has vowed never to make such a monumental mistake again. She expects others to live up to her seriously high standards too!

Most likely to: Keep a cool head when things heat up.

Least likely to: Get caught napping on the job.

Echo

Let's Make Some Noise!

Origin: Echo lived in an undersea kingdom home to a giant oyster shell known as the Pearl of Wisdom. The Pearl was encased in a magic bubble, and when a gang of mean sea horses known as the Aqua Jocks came to town, Echo used her booming voice to blast them away, saving the Pearl and the entire kingdom.

Personality: Echo may seem reserved, but she can be pretty feisty when the time comes for battle. Just ask Gill Grunt. He's the one who made her a Skylander!

Most likely to: Speak her mind. She's pretty good at that.

Least likely to: Whisper. She's not very good at that.

Making Waves!

Origin: Flip Wreck has always loved discovering old shipwrecks and searching for mysteries under the sea. One day, he was swimming in an underwater graveyard when an army of giant Ice Vikings broke free from their netherworld prison and attacked his home. He valiantly chased them away using a homemade suit of armor, and was soon rewarded with membership in the Skylanders.

Personality: Flip Wreck might be the fearless protector of Bottlenose Bay and a hero to his dolphin friends but, don't worry, he doesn't let it go to his head.

Most likely to: Craft a super-cool suit of armor (plus an awesome shield and sword) using stuff from old shipwrecks.

Least likely to: Invite an Ice Viking to a barbecue.

Gill Grunt

Fear the Fish!

Origin: A crack Gillman Marine commando, Gill fell head over flippers in love with a musical mermaid from a misty cloud lagoon. However, his fishy heart was broken when he returned from his tour of duty to discover that his swimming sweetheart had been snatched by pesky pirates. He still searches for her to this day.

Personality: A loyal friend and ally, Gill is as bighearted as he is brave. Just don't ask him to sing. His singing voice sounds like a jellyfish gargling seaweed.

Most likely to: Give bad guys a washing down with his High Pressure Power Hose.

Least likely to: Dry up. He loves telling war stories or waxing lyrical about his lost mermaid.

Punk Shock

Amp It Up!

Origin: The daughter of the king of Wondrous Waters, Punk Shock turned her back on royal life to go hunting with her electric crossbow. All that changed when Snow Trolls put the kingdom on ice. Punk gave those trolls a royal shock!

Personality: A natural rebel. Punk is simply shocking when it comes to being told what to do.

Most likely to: Listen to her highly charged music at MAXIMUM VOLUME!

Least likely to: Act in any way like a princess!

Go Fish!

Origin: It's no wonder Master Eon wanted to recruit Rip Tide. The ferocious fish was the best Aqua-Fighter anyone had ever seen—which was probably why Kaos sent a platoon of Squidface Brutes to take on the underwater champion. Just one platoon? Ha! Rip Tide had them for breakfast.

Personality: Highly adaptable, Rip Tide can master any fighting style in minutes. While you've been reading this, he's perfected Dory Duels, Flounder Fencing, and Sawfish Saber Sparring.

Most likely to: Win! Rip's the finest swords-fish in all of Skylands.

Least likely to: Settle for second best.

Slam Bam

Armed and Dangerous!

Origin: Once upon a time, all Slam Bam wanted was to be left alone crafting ice sculptures and scoffing snow cones on his floating glacier. But that didn't stop Kaos from zapping his home in the hope of discovering the yeti's secret snow-cone ingredient. Slam Bam drifted on a rapidly melting iceberg until washing up at Eon's Citadel, where he trained to become a Skylander.

Personality: Slam Bam can be a little frosty with folks he doesn't know, but soon thaws over time. Get on his bad side, however, and the polar pugilist will knock you out cold.

Most likely to: Put enemies on ice in one of his frozen prisons.

Least likely to: Order red-hot curry!

Wham-Shell

Brace for the Mace!

Origin: The son of Clam King Roland, Wham-Shell was called on to defend his underwater realm when trolls built drilling rigs to pump oil from the ocean bed. As if that wasn't bad enough, the trolls also started plundering Roland's riches in sneaky submarine raids. That is until Wham-Shell smashed them to smithereens using his troll-cracking Malacostracan Mace.

Personality: Regal and heroic, this courageous crustacean never forgets the common clams and protects the seas for all his worth.

Most likely to: Smother foes with sucking Starfish Bullets—if his mace doesn't mash them up first.

Least likely to: Let his gleaming carapace lose its shine.

Ride the Lightning!

Zap

Origin: Always a show-off in the sea, Zap was dragged far from his royal home by a fierce riptide. Lost and alone, the Water Dragon prince was raised by a family of friendly electric eels. To keep up with his adopted brothers and sisters, the bright spark soon created a harness capable of storing an endless supply of crackling electricity.

Personality: Naturally curious and super-competitive, mischievous Zap is also a bit of a prankster, loving to shock his fellow Skylanders whenever he gets a chance.

Most likely to: Spend his spare time surfing on a stream of sparking sea slime.

Least likely to: Slow down and think about what he's doing first.

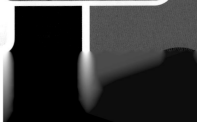

Thumpback

GIANTS

Hail to the Whale!

Origin: Thumpback joined the pirate crew of the Phantom Tide not to pillage and plunder, but to go fishing. Then, one fateful day, the legendary Leviathan Cloud Crab took the bait and pulled Thumpback overboard. The Giant was hauled through the skies, narrowly escaping banishment to the Chest of Exile with the rest of the Phantom Tide's crew.

Personality: Gifted with the patience of an angler, steadfast Thumpback soon realized that his true calling was to protect Skylands as one of the very first Skylanders.

Most likely to: Have a whale of a time by Belly Flopping on foes.

Least likely to: Sing a sea shanty. For a whale Thumpback is remarkably tone deaf.

Keeping It Cool!

Freeze Blade

Origin: Freeze Blade wasn't happy when his family moved from the Frozen Wastelands of Vesh to the Great Lava Lakes. Not only was it swelteringly hot, but there wasn't a scrap of ice for miles around. However, as time passed, the speed skater realized he held an incredible ability to slide on any surface—even red-hot lava.

Personality: Freeze Blade makes friends easily and soon became pals with his hot-headed neighbours. Bullies, however, leave him cold.

Most likely to: Slide into action without a thought for his own personal safety.

Least likely to: Stay in one place for long. He's always on the move.

Freeze Bomb

A sensational combo of chakram chucking and Skunk-Fu. Too much fun!

Freeze Buckler

Send bad guys to a Watery grave with this perfect Elemental match.

Freeze Charge

A great combo for when you want to SWAP but don't want to lose Freeze Blade's trademark Speed.

Freeze Drilla

Here's an idea: fire out a Frostcicle, then finish 'em off with a Banana Split.

Freeze Jet

Fire out some Shaved Ice while careering through the Air. Try it!

Freeze Kraken

Hold on, won't that ice melt? Of course not! See for yourself with this ace switch.

Freeze Loop

Take Kaos down with a Frigid Whirl and a Portable Hole. Magnificent work, Portal Master!

207

Freeze Ranger

Who'd have thought frozen chicken could be so effective?

Freeze Rise

This icy warrior has legs . . . lots of them!

Freeze Rouser

Chakram Throw from above, Deep Dig from below. What a SWAP!

Freeze Shadow

A truly great mix of Water force and Magic Stealth.

Ice to Meet You, snake bottom!

If the ghostly Undead base doesn't send enemies scattering, the Shaved Ice attack will!

Take Freeze Blade for a Jaded Spin – with a little help from Doom Stone.

Friends unite as Freeze Blade teams up with the Skylander who introduced him to Master Eon.

209

Eight Legs and No Pegs!

Wash Buckler

Origin: Adopted by a fearsome band of pirates, Wash Buckler was never comfortable with pirating. All that thieving and plundering and making people walk the plank seemed to be a bit inappropriate. So the Mermasquid taught his pirate peers the error of their ways, transforming them into the most heroic buccaneers you could ever hope to meet.

Personality: Kindhearted and true, this plucky privateer was forced to protect his crew from peeved pirates who thought he was letting their side down.

Most likely to: Blast blackhearted blaggards with his blistering bubble gun.

Least likely to: Take up pillaging.

Wash Blade

It's a swashbuckling, bubble-shooting, ice-skating Mermasquid!

Wash Bomb

Water and Life collide to create this awesome . . . er . . . Mermaskunk?

Wash Charge

Merge the Captain of Piranha Bay with Magna Charge's Magneto Ball.

211

Wash Drilla

Bladesail *and* Explosive Growth? Yes please!

Wash Jet

Ahoy there mateys! This is one ex-pirate who's going Sky Writing!

Wash Kraken

Water on Fire shouldn't work—but it does when it's Wash Kraken.

Wash Loop

Might meets Magic in this collision of some of Skylands' most awesome abilities.

Wash Ranger

Shiver me timbers! Looks like there's an Approaching Storm!

Wash Rise

How about following up Parley Popper with a quick Spyder Mine? Nice, right?

Wash Rouser

Marooned meets Minor Miners with this highly effective Water-Earth SWAP.

Wash Shadow

Give Wash Buckler a Stealth boost with Trap Shadow's mighty Shade Steps.

Wash Shake

Watch out bad guys—there's a Mermasnake in town!

Wash Shift

Fire that Bubble Blaster and open up that Vortex of Doom. This combo never grows old.

Wash Stone

Captain of Piranha Bay meets Spinball King!

Wash Zone

A classic combo that even Wash Buckler's old pirate shipmates would be proud of.

How Complete Is *Your* Collection?

Put a check mark next to all the Skylanders you own!

Series 1 Air

- ☐ Blades
- ☐ Fling Kong
- ☐ Jet-Vac
- ☐ Lightning Rod
- ☐ Pop Thorn
- ☐ Scratch
- ☐ Sonic Boom
- ☐ Warnado
- ☐ Whirlwind

Series 2 Air

- ☐ Lightning Rod
- ☐ Sonic Boom
- ☐ Turbo Jet-Vac
- ☐ Whirlwind

Series 3 Air

- ☐ Full Blast Jet-Vac
- ☐ Horn Blast Whirlwind

Series 1 Earth

- ☐ Bash
- ☐ Dino-Rang
- ☐ Fist Bump
- ☐ Flashwing
- ☐ Prism Break
- ☐ Rocky Roll
- ☐ Scorp
- ☐ Slobber Tooth
- ☐ Terrafin

Series 2 Earth

- ☐ Bash
- ☐ Prism Break
- ☐ Terrafin

215

Series 3 Earth

- ☐ Hyper Beam Prism Break
- ☐ Knockout Terrafin

Series 1 Fire

- ☐ Eruptor
- ☐ Flameslinger
- ☐ Fryno
- ☐ Hot Dog
- ☐ Ignitor
- ☐ Smolderdash
- ☐ Sunburn
- ☐ Torch
- ☐ Trail Blazer

Series 2 Fire

- ☐ Eruptor
- ☐ Fire Bone Hot Dog
- ☐ Flameslinger
- ☐ Hog Wild Fryno
- ☐ Ignitor

Series 3 Fire

- ☐ Lava Barf Eruptor

Series 1 Life

- ☐ Bumble Blast
- ☐ Camo
- ☐ Food Fight
- ☐ High Five
- ☐ Shroomboom
- ☐ Stealth Elf
- ☐ Stump Smash
- ☐ Zook
- ☐ Zoo Lou

Series 2 Life

- ☐ Stealth Elf
- ☐ Stump Smash
- ☐ Sure Shot Shroomboom
- ☐ Thorn Horn Camo
- ☐ Zook

Series 3 Life

- ☐ Ninja Stealth Elf

Series 1 Magic

- ☐ Cobra Cadabra
- ☐ Déjà Vu

☐ Double Trouble

☐ Dune Bug

☐ Pop Fizz

☐ Spyro

☐ Star Strike

☐ Voodood

☐ Wrecking Ball

Series 2 Magic

☐ Double Trouble

☐ Spyro

☐ Super Gulp Pop Fizz

☐ Wrecking Ball

Series 3 Magic

☐ Fizzy Frenzy Pop Fizz

☐ Mega Ram Spyro

Series 1 Tech

☐ Boomer

☐ Chopper

☐ Countdown

☐ Drill Sergeant

☐ Drobot

☐ Sprocket

☐ Tread Head

☐ Trigger Happy

☐ Wind-Up

Series 2 Tech

☐ Drill Sergeant

☐ Drobot

☐ Heavy Duty Sprocket

☐ Trigger Happy

Series 3 Tech

☐ Big Bang Trigger Happy

Series 1 Undead

☐ Bat Spin

☐ Chop Chop

☐ Cynder

☐ Fright Rider

☐ Funny Bone

☐ Ghost Roaster

☐ Grim Creeper

☐ Hex

☐ Roller Brawl

Series 2 Undead

- ☐ Chop Chop
- ☐ Cynder
- ☐ Hex

Series 3 Undead

- ☐ Phantom Cynder
- ☐ Twin Blade Chop Chop

Series 1 Water

- ☐ Chill
- ☐ Echo
- ☐ Flip Wreck
- ☐ Gill Grunt
- ☐ Punk Shock
- ☐ Rip Tide
- ☐ Slam Bam
- ☐ Wham-Shell
- ☐ Zap

Series 2 Water

- ☐ Blizzard Chill
- ☐ Gill Grunt
- ☐ Slam Bam

- ☐ Zap

Series 3 Water

- ☐ Anchors Away Gill Grunt

Series 4 Water

- ☐ Tidal Wave Gill Grunt

Giants

- ☐ Bouncer
- ☐ Crusher
- ☐ Eye-Brawl
- ☐ Hot Head
- ☐ Ninjini
- ☐ Swarm
- ☐ Thumpback
- ☐ Tree Rex

SWAP Force

- ☐ Blast Zone
- ☐ Boom Jet
- ☐ Doom Stone
- ☐ Fire Kraken
- ☐ Free Ranger

- ☐ Freeze Blade
- ☐ Grilla Drilla
- ☐ Hoot Loop
- ☐ Magna Charge
- ☐ Night Shift
- ☐ Rattle Shake
- ☐ Rubble Rouser
- ☐ Spy Rise
- ☐ Stink Bomb
- ☐ Trap Shadow
- ☐ Wash Buckler

Trap Team

- ☐ Blastermind
- ☐ Bushwhack
- ☐ Enigma
- ☐ Gear Shift
- ☐ Gusto
- ☐ Head Rush
- ☐ Jawbreaker
- ☐ Ka-Boom
- ☐ Krypt King
- ☐ Lob-Star

- ☐ Short Cut
- ☐ Snap Shot
- ☐ Thunderbolt
- ☐ Tuff Luck
- ☐ Wallop
- ☐ Wildfire

Minis

- ☐ Barkley
- ☐ Bop
- ☐ Breeze
- ☐ Drobit
- ☐ Eye-Small
- ☐ Gill Runt
- ☐ Hijinx
- ☐ Mini Jini
- ☐ Pet-Vac
- ☐ Small Fry
- ☐ Spry
- ☐ Terrabite
- ☐ Thumpling
- ☐ Trigger Snappy
- ☐ Weeruptor

☐ Whisper Elf

Dark

☐ Dark Blast Zone

☐ Dark Food Fight

☐ Dark Mega Ram Spyro

☐ Dark Slobber Tooth

☐ Dark Snap Shot

☐ Dark Spyro

☐ Dark Stealth Elf

☐ Dark Wash Buckler

☐ Dark Wildfire

LightCore

☐ LightCore Bumble Blast

☐ LightCore Chill

☐ LightCore Countdown

☐ LightCore Drobot

☐ LightCore Eruptor

☐ LightCore Flashwing

☐ LightCore Grim Creeper

☐ LightCore Hex

☐ LightCore Jet-Vac

☐ LightCore Pop Fizz

☐ LightCore Prism Break

☐ LightCore Shroomboom

☐ LightCore Smolderdash

☐ LightCore Star Strike

☐ LightCore Star Strike (Enchanted)

☐ LightCore Warnado

☐ LightCore Wham-Shell

Do you own any other rare or unusual Skylanders?

List them here!

_____

_____

_____

_____

_____

_____

Alphabetical index for Skylanders: The Complete Collection

Barkley 89
Bash................................ 39
Bat Spin 169
Blades.............................13
Blast Blade...................76
Blast Bomb 76
Blast Buckler 76
Blast Charge................77
Blast Drilla...................77
Blast Jet 77
Blast Kraken 77
Blast Loop....................78
Blast Ranger 78
Blast Rise.....................78
Blast Rouser 78
Blast Shadow 79
Blast Shake 79
Blast Shift 79
Blast Stone...................79
Blast Zone 75
Blastermind 113
Boom Blade.................. 24
Boom Bomb 24
Boom Buckler 24
Boom Charge...............25
Boom Drilla..................25
Boom Jet 23
Boom Kraken 25
Boom Loop...................25
Boom Ranger...............26
Boom Rise.................... 26
Boom Rouser 26
Boom Shadow 26
Boom Shake 27
Boom Shift 27
Boom Stone 27
Boom Zone 27
Boomer 143
Bop 37
Bouncer..................... 152
Breeze...........................11
Bumble Blast 91
Bushwhack...................87
Camo............................ 92
Chill.............................195
Chop Chop.................170

Chopper......................144
Cobra Cadabra........... 117
Countdown 145
Crusher 48
Cynder.........................171
Déjà Vu.......................118
Dino Rang 40
Doom Blade 50
Doom Bomb 50
Doom Buckler.............50
Doom Charge...............51
Doom Drilla..................51
Doom Jet 51
Doom Kraken...............51
Doom Loop...................52
Doom Ranger 52
Doom Rise....................52
Doom Rouser...............52
Doom Shadow..............53
Doom Shake 53
Doom Shift...................53
Doom Stone 49
Doom Zone...................53
Double Trouble...........119
Drill Sergeant.............146
Drobit..........................141
Drobot 147
Dune Bug....................120
Echo 196
Enigma 114
Eruptor 65
Eye-Brawl 178
Eye-Small 167
Fire Blade 81
Fire Bomb 81
Fire Buckler 81
Fire Charge...................82
Fire Drilla.....................82
Fire Jet.........................82
Fire Kraken..................80
Fire Loop......................82
Fire Ranger 83
Fire Rise 83
Fire Rouser 83
Fire Shadow 83
Fire Shake 84

Fire Shift 84
Fire Stone.....................84
Fire Zone 84
Fist Bump 41
Flameslinger................ 66
Flashwing 42
Fling Kong 14
Flip Wreck 197
Food Fight 93
Free Blade 29
Free Bomb 29
Free Buckler 29
Free Charge................. 30
Free Drilla................... 30
Free Jet 30
Free Kraken 30
Free Loop.....................31
Free Ranger.................28
Free Rise.....................31
Free Rouser.................31
Free Shadow 31
Free Shake 32
Free Shift 32
Free Stone...................32
Free Zone....................32
Freeze Blade 205
Freeze Bomb.............206
Freeze Buckler 206
Freeze Charge 206
Freeze Drilla 207
Freeze Jet 207
Freeze Kraken............207
Freeze Loop 207
Freeze Ranger 208
Freeze Rise................208
Freeze Rouser...........208
Freeze Shadow 208
Freeze Shake.............209
Freeze Shift 209
Freeze Stone.............209
Freeze Zone 209
Fright Rider 172
Fryno............................67
Funny Bone 173
Gearshift 139
Ghost Roaster...........174

Gill Grunt 198
Gill Runt 193
Grilla Blade 102
Grilla Bomb 102
Grilla Buckler 102
Grilla Charge 103
Grilla Drilla 101
Grilla Jet 103
Grilla Kraken 103
Grilla Loop 103
Grilla Ranger 104
Grilla Rise 104
Grilla Rouser 104
Grilla Shadow 104
Grilla Shake 105
Grilla Shift 105
Grilla Stone 105
Grilla Zone 105
Grim Creeper 175
Gusto 9
Head Rush 35
Hex 176
High Five 94
Hijinx 168
Hoot Blade 128
Hoot Bomb 128
Hoot Buckler 128
Hoot Charge 129
Hoot Drilla 129
Hoot Jet 129
Hoot Kraken 129
Hoot Loop 127
Hoot Ranger 130
Hoot Rise 130
Hoot Rouser 130
Hoot Shadow 130
Hoot Shake 131
Hoot Shift 131
Hoot Stone 131
Hoot Zone 131
Hot Dog 68
Hot Head 74
Ignitor 69
Jawbreaker 140
Jet-Vac 15
Ka-Boom 61
Krypt King 165
Lightning Rod 16
Lob-Star 191
Magna Blade 154
Magna Bomb 154
Magna Buckler 154
Magna Charge 153

Magna Drilla 155
Magna Jet 155
Magna Kraken 155
Magna Loop 155
Magna Ranger 156
Magna Rise 156
Magna Rouser 156
Magna Shadow 156
Magna Shake 157
Magna Shift 157
Magna Stone 157
Magna Zone 157
Mini Jini 115
Night Blade 180
Night Bomb 180
Night Buckler 180
Night Charge 181
Night Drilla 181
Night Jet 181
Night Kraken 181
Night Loop 182
Night Ranger 182
Night Rise 182
Night Rouser 182
Night Shadow 183
Night Shake 183
Night Shift 179
Night Stone 183
Night Zone 183
Ninjini 126
Pet-Vac 12
Pop Fizz 121
Pop Thorn 17
Prism Break 43
Punk Shock 199
Rattle Blade 185
Rattle Bomb 185
Rattle Buckler 185
Rattle Charge 186
Rattle Drilla 186
Rattle Jet 186
Rattle Kraken 186
Rattle Loop 187
Rattle Ranger 187
Rattle Rise 187
Rattle Rouser 187
Rattle Shadow 188
Rattle Shake 184
Rattle Shift 188
Rattle Stone 188
Rattle Zone 188
Rip Tide 200
Rocky Roll 44

Roller Brawl 177
Rubble Blade 55
Rubble Bomb 55
Rubble Buckler 55
Rubble Charge 56
Rubble Drilla 56
Rubble Jet 56
Rubble Kraken 56
Rubble Loop 57
Rubble Ranger 57
Rubble Rise 57
Rubble Rouser 54
Rubble Shadow 57
Rubble Shake 58
Rubble Shift 58
Rubble Stone 58
Rubble Zone 58
Scorp 45
Scratch 18
Short Cut 166
Shroomboom 95
Slam Bam 201
Slobber Tooth 46
Small Fry 63
Smolderdash 70
Snap Shot 192
Sonic Boom 19
Sprocket 148
Spry 116
Spy Blade 159
Spy Bomb 159
Spy Buckler 159
Spy Charge 160
Spy Drilla 160
Spy Jet 160
Spy Kraken 160
Spy Loop 161
Spy Ranger 161
Spy Rise 158
Spy Rouser 161
Spy Shadow 161
Spy Shake 162
Spy Shift 162
Spy Stone 162
Spy Zone 162
Spyro 122
Star Strike 123
Stealth Elf 96
Stink Blade 107
Stink Bomb 106
Stink Buckler 107
Stink Charge 107
Stink Drilla 108

Stink Jet......................108
Stink Kraken 108
Stink Loop..................108
Stink Ranger...............109
Stink Rise...................109
Stink Rouser..............109
Stink Shadow.............109
Stink Shake.................110
Stink Shift...................110
Stink Stone 110
Stink Zone...................110
Stump Smash..............97
Sunburn........................71
Swarm...........................22
Terrabite.................... 38
Terrafin 47
Thumpback............ 204
Thumpling..................194
Thunderbolt.................10
Torch 72
Trail Blazer 73
Trap Blade..................133
Trap Bomb 133
Trap Buckler 133
Trap Charge................134
Trap Drilla...................134
Trap Jet......................134
Trap Kraken 134
Trap Loop...................135
Trap Ranger................135
Trap Rise....................135
Trap Rouser 135
Trap Shadow..............132
Trap Shake 136
Trap Shift...................136
Trap Stone..................136
Trap Zone...................136
Tread Head 149
Tree Rex 100
Trigger Happy.............150
Trigger Snappy..........142
Tuff Luck..................... 88
Voodood.....................124
Wallop 36
Warnado 20
Wash Blade................. 211
Wash Bomb 211
Wash Buckler..............210
Wash Charge.............. 211
Wash Drilla..................212
Wash Jet 212
Wash Kraken 212
Wash Loop..................212

Wash Ranger.............. 213
Wash Rise...................213
Wash Rouser.............. 213
Wash Shadow............213
Wash Shake................214
Wash Shift..................214
Wash Stone 214
Wash Zone..................214
Weeruptor 64
Wham-Shell..............202
Whirlwind.....................21
Whisper Elf.................90
Wildfire...................... 62
Wind-Up 151
Wrecking Ball............125
Zap.............................203
Zoo Lou....................... 99
Zook 98